LET'S FIND OUT ABOUT

DOGS

BARBARA HEHNER

Random House
Toronto

Acknowledgements
Many thanks to the following people who generously shared their
expertise with me: Joan Henry, Education Officer with the
Toronto Humane Society, Sylvia Sharp of National Public
Relations, Mike Randall of the North American Flyball
Association, Elsie Chadwick, and Rick Archbold.

Dedication: To Joshua, who wants to live in harmony with the
Earth and all its creatures

Published in Canada in 1991 by Random House of Canada Limited, Toronto.

Canadian Cataloguing in Publication Data

Hehner, Barbara
  Let's find out about dogs

ISBN 0–394–22086–2

1. Dogs – Juvenile literature. I. Title.

SF426.5.H44 1990   j636.7   C90-094329-7

COVER AND TEXT DESIGN: Brant Cowie/ArtPlus Limited
EDITOR: Lillian Goodman
ART DIRECTION: Lorraine Smith/ArtPlus Limited
PAGE MAKE UP: Valerie Phillips/ArtPlus Limited
TYPE OUTPUT: TypeLine Express Limited
ILLUSTRATIONS: Janet Wilson
COVER PHOTO: Peter Paterson

Printed and bound in Canada

Contents

The Long Partnership

How They Met

Long, long ago, as far back as the earliest drawings human beings made on rocks, as far back as the earliest tales they told around their fires, dogs and people were together. One ancient legend explains their special friendship.

When the world was new, the earth suddenly split open. A human being was stranded alone on one side of the deep chasm. All the animals were on the other side. Only the dog saw the gap widening and made a mighty leap across it. But the dog didn't quite make it. It clung desperately to the edge of the chasm with its front paws. Then the human being reached down and rescued the dog. Since that day, says the legend, people and dogs have been close, devoted friends.

Human beings have had a longer, closer relationship with dogs than with any other animal. The bond probably goes back at least 15,000 years, but it began in a way that might surprise you. The animal that made the leap to join human beings wasn't yet a dog. It was a wolf.

In those long-ago times, human beings had a hard life. Their homes were caves or very simple shelters. They had fires to warm themselves and they had a few tools. They didn't yet know how to grow their own food. They gathered nuts and berries, and small groups hunted with spears and bows and arrows. Hunting was tiring and dangerous, since many of the animals the hunters chased were stronger and bigger than they were.

Like the human hunters, wolves hunted in packs to bring down larger prey. Since the wolves chased the same food that human beings wanted, how did these rivals ever become friends? Here's how it may have happened.

When the hunt went well, the people had more meat than they could eat all at once. There were also some leftovers that their jaws weren't strong enough to chew.

Wolves may have come close to their campsites to steal the meaty bones they left. At first, people may have tried to drive the wolves away. Then they noticed that the wolves got rid of their garbage before it rotted and smelled. The wolves also had keen senses of hearing and smell. They knew that enemies were approaching before the people did. If the wolves made a lot of noise, the people had time to defend themselves. So the wolves were allowed to remain nearby.

It may have happened that the children found some orphaned wolf cubs and raised the animals themselves. As these children grew up, they began to go hunting, and their tame wolves tagged along. The hunters soon discovered that when they lost the trail of a deer or an antelope, the wolves could still track their prey by scent. They could race ahead and hold an animal at bay until the hunters arrived to kill it.

3

As time went by, people noticed that some animals were better trackers than others. Some were faster, stronger runners. Some were more willing to accept a human being as the pack leader. People began to select animals with the skills they wanted and mate the males and females. If they were lucky, they would get pups with the same qualities. This is how the breeding of dogs began.

Scientists can tell from the bones left behind at ancient campsites that these dogs began to look different from wolves. Their jaws became weaker and their fangs weren't as long. While a weak-jawed wolf would quickly die, a weak-jawed dog who was a wonderful tracker would be fed and protected. It could survive to produce more like itself. Some dogs began to have rounder muzzles and floppy ears. This made them look puppyish, even when they were grown up. People long ago seem to have found this as charming as we do today. If a puppy was born with a feature that made it look special, such as a curly tail or a longer coat, the owner would probably try to breed more like it. (People are still doing this today, and creating new breeds.)

When human beings learned how to grow crops and raise sheep and cattle, about 10,000 years ago, dogs became even more useful. Now dogs helped them guard their crops and herd their animals.

All the earliest civilizations of the world have left statues, carvings, or pictures of dogs. Often they look very similar to breeds we know today. A golden fan more than 3000 years old shows an Egyptian pharaoh hunting ostriches. His sleek greyhounds are running beside his chariot. A 2500-year-old stone sculpture from Assyria (part of present-day Iraq) shows huge mastiffs on a lion hunt. Over a thousand years ago in China, emperors bred tiny dogs much like today's Pekingeses. The dogs sat in the wide sleeves of their silk robes and helped to keep them warm in cold weather!

Heavenly Dogs

When you look up at the sky on a winter night in North America, the brightest star you can see is Sirius. It is often called the Dog Star, because it is in the *constellation* (star grouping) called *Canis Major*. (These are the Latin words for "big dog.") In Ancient Egypt, people celebrated the New Year when Sirius rose in the sky. The Dog Star appeared at the same time the Nile River flooded, watering the land so new crops could grow.

The ancient Greeks and Romans called the time when Sirius is closest to the sun, in July and August, the Dog Days. This was the hottest time of year, and they believed that Sirius was adding its heat to the heat of the sun. (This isn't true, of course. Sirius is about twice as hot as our sun, but it is 540,000 times farther away from us!) Today, we still call very hot weather "dog days."

The Cherokee Indians called the Milky Way "where the dog ran." They told a story of some people who noticed that their cornmeal was being stolen every night. They hid to find out who was taking it. They discovered that a little dog was stealing the meal. The people chased him, but he ran up into the sky. The cornmeal on the dog's paws left a trail across the night sky, and this became the stars of the Milky Way.

An old Chinese legend tells of the time when the world was being created. As the stars were being fitted into the heavens, little pieces of blue sky fell to earth. Dogs licked them up. And that is how Chow Chow dogs got their strange blue tongues!

A Record Book For Your Dog

Start when your dog is a puppy, and make a record of its life in words and pictures.

You'll Need:
a scrapbook or photo album

Pictures

1. Take photos of your dog. Ask someone else in the family to take pictures of you with your dog, too. To take good photographs, get down to your pet's level. Pictures of your dog's face are more interesting than pictures of the top of its head! Try to photograph your dog against a plain background so that the dog will stand out clearly. (And, if your dog ever gets lost, you'll be very glad you have a clear picture for a lost poster. See p. 84.)
2. Make some drawings or paintings of your dog. You can learn a lot about your pet's body and movements this way. How long are its ears compared to the size of its head? At what angle does it carry its tail? How is the dog's body curled when it's asleep?
3. Draw a comic strip to show something funny or dramatic that happened to your dog. Remember the time your dog chased the neighbor's cat up a tree? Or the first time it caught a Frisbee? You could even create a comic strip about your pet, "Superdog!"

Words

1. Write a few lines to describe big events in your dog's life, such as learning to walk on a leash, its first visit to the veterinarian, a vacation at the cottage, and so on.
2. Most dogs, whether they're purebred or not, have "papers" of some kind. They probably have health records that show when they had their vaccinations and wormings. If they're purebred, they'll have registration papers and *pedigrees* (family trees). If you keep these documents in your dog's record book, everyone will know exactly where to find them when they're needed. (If your parents want to store these records somewhere else, make photocopies for your dog book.)
3. Read about your dog's breed. You may be surprised to find out that dogs who look like yours once hunted with Egyptian pharaohs, or nestled inside the silk sleeves of Chinese empresses. You may learn that your dog's breed once carried messages on battlefields or saved sailors from drowning. Write something about the history of your dog's breed in its book.
4. Write a poem about your dog and add it to the book, too.

Good Sports

The Saluki may be the oldest dog breed of all. Called El Hor, "the noble one," by the desert sheiks of Arabia, the fleet-footed Saluki was used to hunt gazelle. The Saluki appears on Egyptian murals from 5,000 years ago, looking just as it does today: lean and long-legged, with feathery-looking, droopy ears.

The Saluki is one of a class of dogs called *hounds*. Hounds were first bred for hunting. Sometimes the animals they hunted were used for food, but more often, the hunt was an exciting sport for kings and nobles.

Sight hounds are streamlined dogs with deep chests, long noses, and long, powerful legs. They use their keen eyesight to search out their prey and then run swiftly and silently to overtake it. Afghan Hounds, with their silky long hair to protect them from the cold, once hunted snow leopards in the mountains of Afghanistan. Borzois were used for hundreds of years by Russian royalty to hunt wolves. They worked in pairs to seize the wolf's neck and ear, holding the struggling animal until the hunters arrived.

Scent hounds are the champion sniffers of the dog world. Most of them are sturdy dogs with floppy ears. In fact, the ears of some scent hounds trail on the ground, where they stir up smells for the dog's keen nose to find. Bloodhounds are the best trackers. Perhaps because of their name, some people think bloodhounds are fierce animals. But when they catch up with someone, they're a lot more likely to lick the person's face than bite. Their name comes from the time when only the nobility, "the bluebloods," were allowed to own them.

People have bred scent hounds with different characteristics to hunt particular animals. Otterhounds, strong swimmers with oily waterproof coats, were once used in England to hunt otters for sport. Dachshunds, with their short legs and very long "sausage" bodies, could follow badgers and foxes right into the tunnels of their dens. Little Beagles could pursue rabbits into the underbrush. Most scent hounds have become family pets, but Foxhounds are still used mainly for hunting. They are faster runners than most scent hounds, and excel at working in a pack.

Spaniels, setters, retrievers and *pointers* were all developed as bird-hunting dogs. Spaniels take their name from the country of Spain, where they were first bred. Spaniels *flush* game birds (startle them so that they flutter out of their hiding places), and then retrieve them after the hunter shoots them. Spaniels can fight their way through dense underbrush where people can't go. Hundreds of years ago, the smaller spaniels were called "cocking" or "cocker" spaniels because they were mainly used to hunt woodcock. The bigger spaniels were called "springers" because their job was springing forward to flush birds so they could be captured by greyhounds, falcons, or nets. Spaniels, especially Cocker Spaniels, have become very popular family pets, because they are playful, friendly with children, and easy to train.

Pointer

9

Pointers were first bred in the 1700s, when hunters began to kill game with guns. Pointers race ahead of the hunters, holding their heads high and sniffing the air for the scent of birds. When they find a grouse or partridge, they freeze into a "point" position. They raise one paw, stretch their heads forward in the direction of the bird, and hold their tails out stiffly. The dogs will hold this tense pose until the hunter tells them it's okay to "break" or relax. Hunters tell tall tales about coming upon the skeleton of a lost pointer, still pointing at the skeleton of a bird!

Setters were once called "setting spaniels." Their special job was to "set" or crouch low to the ground near the birds so that hunters could drop a net over them. Later, when hunters began to use guns, setters were bred to point. Most dog lovers agree that setters, with their silky coats, are especially beautiful animals. Irish Setters have red coats, Gordon Setters are black and reddish-brown, while English Setters are white with black or brown spots. When these dogs are kept as pets, they need lots of outdoor exercise.

When hunting ducks with guns became popular in the 1800s, hunters needed a new kind of dog. They wanted a strong swimmer who would plunge into the water and bring back birds they had shot. They developed various breeds of retriever, including the Labrador Retriever, the Chesapeake Bay Retriever, and the Golden Retriever. All these dogs have dense coats that protect them from the chill of the water.

For hundreds of years, the ancestors of the Labrador Retriever were working dogs on the fishing boats of Newfoundland. It was too dangerous for the boats to come in close to the rocky coast. Instead, the dogs would jump into the water and gather up the ends of the fish-filled nets in their mouths. Then they'd battle through the rough waves until they reached the shore. Men waiting there would drag in the nets. British visitors to Newfoundland took the dogs back to England and developed them into hunting dogs. Today, Golden Retrievers and Labrador Retrievers are most often found retrieving balls and Frisbees. They are good-natured, energetic pets.

SURPRISING FACTS ABOUT DOGS

Standing On Guard

Did you know that Canada has four dog breeds all its own? The best known is the huge, furry Newfoundland dog. These dogs are famous for their strength and their lifesaving skills. They have pulled hundreds of drowning people from the water. Dog lovers in Newfoundland believe that the ancestors of these dogs came to their shores with the Vikings, almost 1000 years ago.

The Nova Scotia Duck Tolling Retriever, like other retrievers, was bred for hunting. But it has a hunting style like no other dog. The dog twirls and frolics along the shoreline. Curious ducks swim closer to watch the dog's antics. (Tolling comes from the old English word *tollen*, meaning "lure" or "attract.") Then the hunters rise out of their *blinds* (hiding places) and shoot the ducks. Tolling is not taught; it's a talent these dogs are born with.

Newfoundland Dog

Nova Scotia Duck Tolling Retriever Dog

11

Canadian Eskimo Dogs worked for the Inuit people for almost 2000 years. In winter they pulled sleds, and in summer they carried backpacks. They are strong, thick-coated dogs who can work outside even in freezing temperatures. In recent years, the people of Canada's North switched to snowmobiles, and the Eskimo Dog breed began to die out. By the 1970s, there were only about 200 left. Then a man named William Carpenter started a breeding program for the dogs and they're becoming popular again.

It may be too late to rescue Canada's rarest dog breed, the Tahltan Bear Dog. The Tahltan people of Northwest British Columbia used these small, fearless dogs to help them hunt bears, lynxes, and porcupines. The dogs' loud yodelling barks would hold the animals at bay until the hunters caught up to them. By 1984 the Canadian Kennel Club knew of only two living Bear Dogs, both females who could not have puppies. Dog fanciers still hope to find some of the dogs in a remote area and breed them again.

Eskimo Dog

Tahltan Bear Dog

Digger On Patrol

The new employee at Pearson International Airport in Toronto walked quietly through the crowded baggage area. Seeing his green Agriculture Canada jacket, people stepped aside for him as he went about his work. Finally he found what he was looking for — a suitcase that smelled like salami! Digger the Beagle sat down beside the suitcase and pawed it. His human handler marked the bag with a tag so that it would be searched when its owner took it through customs. And Digger got a dog biscuit.

Digger had more than five months of training before he started work in the summer of 1990. He learned to detect 75 different plant and animal scents, and then he joined Agriculture Canada's Beagle Brigade. Angus, of Vancouver International Airport, and Fred, of Mirabelle Airport near Montreal, are two other members of the team. Angus, the most senior member, has been at work since 1986. Agriculture Canada chose Beagles because they have keen noses, they can concentrate on their work even with a hubbub around them, and they're small dogs who don't frighten the passengers.

Every month, the dogs find about 90 kg (200 lbs.) of plants, meats, and fruit that people are trying to smuggle into Canada. These products could spread diseases to Canadian crops and livestock. Sometimes there are even live animals. These are often endangered species that should not have been taken from their home countries.

Terriers and Toys

People who don't know much about dogs sometimes think all small breeds are pampered lap dogs. In fact, there is as much variety among little dogs as among the bigger breeds. Some small dogs, such as Miniature Poodles and Shih Tzus, were once treasured pets that only royalty could own. Terriers, though, were first bred as fiery, fearless hunters.

In the British Isles, hundreds of years ago, only kings and nobles were allowed to own hounds. But farmers and other common people had their own hunting dogs, the terriers. Their name came from *terra*, the Latin word for "earth," because terriers would dig into tunnels and burrows to chase their prey. Terriers such as Sealyhams and Lakelands were bred to attack and kill *vermin*. These were the small animals that farmers hated because they tore up their fields, ate their crops, or stole their chickens. It took great courage for terriers to bolt into black, narrow passages where they would meet desperate, sharp-toothed and clawed ferrets, badgers, rats, and foxes. Some terriers, such as Fox Terriers and Welsh Terriers, even became popular with wealthy people, who took them along on their fox hunts. If the Foxhounds were baffled by a fox who took refuge in a burrow, the Fox Terriers would go in after it.

Scotland's terriers have been around for at least 500 years. There are Scottish Terriers (Scotties), West Highland White Terriers (Westies), Skye Terriers, and Cairn Terriers. All of them have short, sturdy legs and square, strong jaws. Cairn Terriers got their name because they were small enough to chase rats between the cracks of crumbling rock piles called cairns. (In the movie version of *The Wizard of Oz*, Dorothy's brave little dog Toto is played by a Cairn Terrier.) All the Scottish Terriers make great pets for people who admire their independent spirit.

A few breeds of terrier were developed especially for bloodthirsty contests that people once watched for entertainment. Bull Terriers, a cross between bulldogs and terriers, fought to the death against bulls, badgers, and other dogs. The Manchester Terrier was bred as a rat killer. At one time it worked on farms, but later ratting became a contest that people would watch and bet money on. A Manchester named Billy once killed 100 rats in 6 minutes and 13 seconds.

Tiny Yorkshire Terriers, with their flowing hair and ribbons, look as if they've always sat on silk cushions. But they were first bred to be rat catchers in the coal mines and cotton mills of Northern England. Miners also staged rat-killing contests with their favorite Yorkies. Today these dogs, like other terriers, are much gentler than their ancestors.

Most national kennel clubs, including Canada's, group the tiniest terriers with other very small dogs in a category called "toys." Many of these dogs were developed by breeding the extra-small puppies that are sometimes born in litters of regular-sized dogs. In this way, people produced toy-sized versions of greyhounds, poodles, and spaniels. Pomeranians are tiny relatives of northern dogs such as Samoyeds and Siberian Huskies.

The Italian Greyhound, only about 33 cm (13 ins.) high at the shoulder, has a long, romantic history. The *mummy* (preserved body) of a tiny greyhound has been found in the tomb of an ancient Egyptian pharaoh. The Egyptian Queen Cleopatra liked to surround herself with these slim, graceful dogs. Roman soldiers who conquered Egypt brought the dogs to Italy.

Signs that say "Cave canem" (Beware of the dog) have been found in the ruins of the ancient Roman city of Pompeii. Some people believe that this *doesn't* mean "Watch out, our dog might bite you." Instead, it may mean "Be careful you don't step on our little greyhound!" As the

Romans invaded one European country after another, they took these dogs with them. For hundreds of years, Italian Greyhounds were the pets of the rich. Many famous artists included the elegant dogs in their paintings and sculptures.

For hundreds of years, only the Chinese Imperial family was allowed to own Pekingeses. The family had thousands of these dogs by the early 1800s, and thousands of servants looked after them. The common people had to bow to the dogs, and anyone caught trying to steal one was executed. In 1860, British soldiers attacked Peking and took over the Imperial Palace. The defenders killed their Pekingeses rather than have them fall into the hands of their enemies. But a British soldier found several little dogs cowering behind a curtain and brought them back to England for Queen Victoria.

The world's smallest dog, the round-headed, big-eyed Chihuahua, is also one of the most mysterious. Some people believe that the Chihuahua was first developed by the ancient peoples of Mexico, the Aztecs and the Toltecs. Others say that there were no dogs in Mexico until the Spanish arrived in 1519. Still others say that Chinese dog breeders brought the tiny dogs to Mexico only about 100 years ago. Most Chihuahuas weigh between 1 and 2.75 kg (2 to 6 lbs.). However, an American Chihuahua named Peanuts weighs only 630 g (1 lb., 6 oz.)!

Lion-Hearted Lhasas

They look like cute little toys, especially when they wear ribbons to keep their long hair out of their eyes. But Lhasa Apsos are one of the world's oldest dog breeds, and they're used to getting a lot of respect. For 2000 years, these dogs were cared for by Buddhist monks in the sacred city of Lhasa, Tibet, high in the Himalaya Mountains. They were known as *Apso Seng Kye,* the Barking Lion Sentinel Dog. Alert and courageous despite their small size, they guarded monasteries and royal palaces. The *lamas* (monks) thought that Lhasa Apsos looked like lions, the animal protectors of Buddha. One legend said that lamas who died would sometimes be *reincarnated* (reborn) as Lhasa Apsos.

Only the highest ranking people in Tibet could own these brave little dogs. They were thought to bring good luck and were never sold. From time to time, though, they were given as presents to honored foreign guests. This is how Lhasa Apsos finally made their way to Europe and North America in the 1920s and 1930s.

For a Biscuit, a Bed, and a Pat On the Head

A flock of plump, white sheep flows down over a green hillside in England. Behind them, keeping them on the move, is a tireless dog, a Border Collie. The dog runs back and forth, barking, heading off the sheep who are trying to stray. If the sheep stop, the dog crouches low and moves in close to them, staring at them so hard that they start moving again. Sheep herders call this special staring skill "the eye." The dog controls the sheep without panicking them into a stampede. In the British Isles, Australia, and other countries, Border Collies have been doing this job for hundreds of years.

Today, most dogs are family pets rather than working animals. But in the past, most people could not afford to keep dogs unless they could do something useful. Here are just a few of the other jobs dogs have done.

18 Border Collie

Dogs In Sheep's Clothing

When European explorers arrived on the coast of British Columbia in the 1700s, they saw many things that impressed them. The native people lived in huge cedar-plank houses. They carved tall totem poles. And the Coast Salish people had something else that surprised the explorers. They had small, white, woolly dogs that the Salish women sheared like sheep. The women wove the wool into soft, warm blankets.

By the late 1800s, though, the Coast Salish people were using blankets that had come from Europe as trade goods. Their special dog breed died out. Luckily, we can still see what the dogs looked like. The artist Paul Kane visited the Salish villages in the 1840s. He put one of the little white dogs in a corner of a painting called "Cla-lum Women Weaving a Blanket." You can see it if you go to the Royal Ontario Museum in Toronto.

All the countries that ring the Arctic Circle have strong, thick-coated, wolfish-looking dogs who can work in the coldest weather. The Samoyeds of Siberia have magnificent, thick white coats. Siberian Huskies have mixed coat colors, with a pattern on their faces that makes them look as if they're always smiling. For centuries these dogs were sled-pullers and reindeer herders. In the North American Arctic, the Alaskan Malamute and the Canadian Eskimo Dog pulled Inuit sleds and helped them hunt polar bears and wolves. Today, snowmobiles have replaced sled dogs, but these breeds are still popular as pets. In snowy parts of North America, people still race the dogs for fun.

Saint Bernards were probably the first dogs specially trained to rescue people. More than 1000 years ago, a monk named Father Bernard started a *hospice* (a place to rest and get food) in a mountain pass in the Swiss Alps. Later, the monks began to keep Saint Bernard dogs to guard the hospice and to help find lost travelers. Often, the monks sent out several dogs to search for a missing person. When they found him, one or two of the dogs would lie down beside him to keep him warm. One would lick the person's face to keep him awake, and another would run back to the hospice for help. Barry, a Saint Bernard who lived at the beginning of the 1800s, rescued 40 people and became famous all over Europe. Today, lighter, faster dogs like German Shepherds have taken over much of the mountain rescue work. But Saint Bernards make fine pets for families with the space to house these gentle giants.

The black, broad-chested Rottweiler was once known as the "butcher's dog of Rottweil." (Rottweil is a town in Germany.) When the Rottweil butchers went on cattle-buying trips, they needed strong, trustworthy dogs to herd the cattle and protect them from robbers. They tied their leather money pouches around the Rottweilers' necks, knowing that no one would dare to remove them. Today, hardworking Rottweilers are guard dogs and police dogs in many European countries.

German Shepherds started out as sheepherders, but they have probably done more different kinds of work than any other dog breed. They are strong, intelligent dogs who follow commands well. In many countries, German Shepherds work as army dogs, guard dogs, and police dogs. They are used to sniff out terrorist bombs and smuggled drugs. They track criminals and disarm them when they find them, and they find disaster victims under rubble, mud, or snow. German Shepherds also work as guide dogs for the blind.

Because dogs have been our closest animal companions, they have been included in the ugliest parts of human life as well as the most pleasant. Long ago, armies fought each other on horseback. Huge Mastiffs were sent into battle wearing spiked collars to slash the enemy soldiers and their horses. Even in recent wars, dogs have been used to carry messages and supplies on battlefields or go on night patrol.

From ancient times until the mid-1800s, there were cruel "baiting" contests in which dogs were forced to fight to the death with bears, bulls, and lions. Today, even though these contests are illegal in most places, "pit bulls" are still bred for brutal dog fights. Some communities have tried to make laws to ban these dogs. It's very hard, though, to judge what a pit bull really is. The American and Staffordshire Bull Terriers are usually the breeds that are banned, but people who breed these dogs protest that they are no longer fierce fighters. Pit bulls, they point out, can be a mixture of several breeds. Their owners breed the most vicious dogs they can find, then train them to be even more vicious. Many dog breeds can, and do, become dangerous if treated this way.

Firehouse Dogs

No one knows the earliest history of the spotted dogs called Dalmatians. Some people who study dog breeds think the Romany people, who are also known as gypsies, kept these dogs. In the Middle Ages, the Romanies travelled from India into Europe, to the part of Yugoslavia called Dalmatia. They took their dogs with them. When wealthy Englishmen passed through Dalmatia on their travels, they may have admired these dogs and brought them back to their own country.

We know that by the 1700s Dalmatians were a familiar sight in England. Their job was to run beside a coach when their noble owners went on a journey. Their barking would warn animals and other vehicles to get off the road. The Dalmatians were also protection against highway robbers. These long-legged dogs were ideal for this work because they were strong, fast runners, and they were not afraid of horses.

In the early 1900s, Dalmatians put their talents to work for fire departments in Canada and the United States. In those days, fire engines were pulled by horses. The dogs ran ahead of the engines, barking to warn people to get out of the way. Once they arrived at the fire, they helped to find and rescue fire victims. When fire departments switched to gasoline-powered engines that went much faster than horses, the Dalmatians were out of a job. However, many fire departments still keep a Dalmatian as a mascot and have pictures of Dalmatian dogs in their fire safety booklets.

THE HUSKY EXPRESS

How would you like to send someone a letter that was carried on a sled pulled by Siberian Huskies? Every winter, dog teams make a mail run from Humphrey, Ontario to Rosseau, Ontario. Your letter will be in a special envelope with a picture of a Husky and the words "Carried by Dog Team" printed on it. When the dogs arrive in Rosseau, a postmark will be put on by hand at the local post office. Then it will be mailed anywhere in the world, even back to you, if you like. (If you are a stamp collector, the envelope will be an unusual addition to your collection.)

What to Do:
Write the letter you want to send. It must be only one or two pages long. On a separate piece of paper, print the complete address of the person you want to send the letter to. Be sure to print clearly and carefully. Put all the papers in an envelope, along with $2.00. Then address the envelope to:

Mrs. Elsie Chadwick
3 Faludon Court
Etobicoke, Ontario
M9B 1J4

Mrs. Chadwick will put your letter in one of the special envelopes. She will address it for you and put the right postage on it. Remember, it can go anywhere in the world.

Important:
The mail run is held in the middle of February every year. Send your letter and $2.00 to Mrs. Chadwick *only in the month of January.* Your letter must arrive at Mrs. Chadwick's *by January 31,* so it won't miss the sled!

A Race Against Death

In the winter of 1925, the 1400 people of Nome, Alaska were facing an epidemic of diphtheria. Several children were already sick, and the town had no serum to protect people from the disease. They sent out desperate telegrams begging for help.

In those days, sled dogs were used in the North to carry supplies and mail. They were also raced for fun and excitement. Some of the fastest teams and their drivers started working in relays to carry the life-saving serum from Anchorage to Nome. Each man and his team of about seven dogs raced 40 to 50 km (30 to 40 miles), then passed the serum on to the next team.

On one stretch, the temperature plunged to -53°C (-63°F). When two of his dogs began to freeze, Charlie Evans bundled them onto his sled. Then he ran in front of the sled to help his remaining dogs pull the load. On the last leg of the run, Gunnar Kaason ran into a blizzard so blinding that he couldn't even see his dogs. But the lead dog, Balto, somehow kept the team on the trail and brought them all safely to Nome. In all, 20 drivers and more than 100 dogs covered 1085 km (674 miles) of frozen wilderness in six days. The town of Nome was saved!

Best Friends

Barney, a Belgian Malinois, is Michael's service dog, and his closest companion. A few years ago, Michael was paralyzed in a car accident. But Michael, a university teacher, can still live on his own with Barney's help. Every morning, Barney carries in the morning newspaper and the mail. If Michael drops something, even an object as small as a dime, Barney picks it up for him. He can pull Michael's wheelchair and help him get in and out of it. When he and Michael come home in the evening, Barney goes in the door first and turns on the lights. One day, Michael felt very sick and needed an ambulance. Barney brought him the cordless telephone and Michael called for help. When the ambulance attendants arrived, they were amazed to find Barney opening the front door for them!

Well-trained dogs are now making life better for people who can't see or hear, for people like Michael who have trouble getting around, and for people in hospitals and other institutions who are lonely and depressed. The idea that dogs could help people this way isn't new. A Chinese scroll from 700 years ago shows a dog guiding a blind man. But it's only in the last 75 years that organized programs to train these dogs have been set up.

German Shepherds were trained to guide German soldiers who had been blinded in World War I. Americans who saw this work in Germany helped to organize the first training school in the United States. They called the school Seeing Eye Inc., and now people often call guide dogs "seeing eye dogs." Today there are 11 guide dog programs in the United States and three in Canada. Not every person who is visually impaired needs or wants a dog. The person must like dogs, of course, and want to care for one. The person must also have a fairly active life, because the dog needs exercise.

Guide dogs must be medium-sized. They have to be big enough for their owners to reach the harness they wear, and strong enough to pull them away from danger. But they must be small enough to sit under desks or restaurant tables, or in the aisles of buses and trains. They have to be smart, able to go out in all kinds of weather, and calm even in crowded and noisy places. They must have good judgment. Sometimes they should *not* obey an order because they can see that it will put their owner in danger. Three dog breeds meet these standards especially well: German Shepherds, Labrador Retrievers, and Golden Retrievers.

In most guide dog programs, puppies are raised with families who give them their first training. The dogs learn to love and trust people. At the same time they learn how to ride on trains and buses, how to go into stores and restaurants, and how to walk on busy streets. When they're between 11 and 18 months old, they go back to the school for training before they meet their new owners. As well as the usual dog commands, they have to learn some special skills. One of the hardest things for guide dogs to learn is to watch out for low-hanging signs and branches. The dogs can walk underneath these hazards, but instead they must lead their people safely around them.

In recent years, dogs have also become useful helpers for people who have little or no hearing. There are now training programs in the United States and Canada for hearing ear dogs. The dogs must be friendly and intelligent, but they don't have to be big or strong. Small, alert, energetic dogs, such as mixed-breed terriers and poodles, are often used, because they can live in small homes and apartments.

Hearing ear dogs are taught to do all kinds of things to help their owners and to save them from danger. For instance, the dogs might lick or nuzzle them awake when their alarm clock goes off. They can also let the person know that the phone or doorbell is ringing, that the baby is crying, or that the fire alarm is sounding. The dogs are taught to keep going from the person to the thing making the sound, back and forth, until the person does something about it.

If you have a dog, you know how much your pet can cheer you up after you've had a bad day. Dogs don't care if you struck out or failed a test; they think you're great, anyway. In the last few years, many studies have been done on people and their pets. Researchers have found that pet owners tend to live longer than people who don't have pets. While people are stroking a dog or cat, their blood pressure goes down and their heart rate slows. People who are sad and too depressed to speak to anyone will sometimes cheer up and begin to talk if they are given a dog to pet. Many hospitals and senior citizens' homes now arrange for people in the community to bring in their pets for regular visits.

Wild Goose Chase

The Aleutian Canada Goose nests on only three Arctic islands. A group of *biologists* (scientists who study living things) wanted to study the geese and figure out ways to help them survive. They had just one problem. They couldn't find the geese! The biologists often fell and hurt themselves as they tried to track the birds through rough brush country. When the birds hid in tall grass, the biologists couldn't see them. Border Collies were brought to the rescue. These dogs can sniff out the birds no matter where they're hiding. Then they use their special staring "eye" to stop the birds in their tracks. The Border Collies round up the geese just like sheep on a ranch. Then the biologists count them, take a good look at them, give them medical care if they need it, and let them go.

Courageous Canines

Most Newfoundland dogs love to plunge into a lake or the sea for a swim. But Shana, a 50 kg (110 lb.) Newfoundland who belonged to a Calgary couple, was different. She had always been afraid of the water. Then a freak storm hit Calgary and icy floodwaters poured down Shana's street. As Shana's owner, Dorothy Laurin, fled from her flooded house, she slipped off the porch steps. Soon she was floundering helplessly in the swift-running water. Shana, overcoming her fear, plunged in to save her. With Dorothy clinging to her neck, Shana swam to higher ground, where human rescuers pulled them to safety.

For over 20 years, the Ralston Purina Company has honored heroic dogs like Shana. There have been dogs who warned of fires, dogs who held off attacking bears and rabid foxes, and dogs who saved their owners from robbers and other criminals. Any animals, not just dogs, who have shown great bravery or loyalty can become members of the Purina Animal Hall of Fame. If you know of an animal who recently did something brave to help people, Ralston Purina would like to hear from you. Write and tell them all about it at this address:

Animal Hall of Fame
Ralston Purina Canada Inc.
2500 Royal Windsor Drive
Mississauga, Ontario
L5J 1K8

Don't Forget:
Print your name and address clearly on your letter, so that Ralston Purina can send you a reply.

Barking Up the Family Tree

About 40 million years ago, a little animal that looked something like a weasel or a mink climbed trees, dug dens to live in, and hunted other animals. If you passed a small animal like this in a zoo today, you might not look twice at it. Instead, you might hurry on to look at the polar bears or tigers. But this animal, called *Miacis*, was something new and important. It was the first true meat-eating mammal, or *carnivore*. All the carnivores in the world today, including seals, bears, raccoons, cats, and dogs, can trace their origins back to Miacis.

As you can tell, the family tree had to branch a few times between Miacis and the dog family we know today. The earliest animal that looked dog-like roamed the forests of the earth about 15 million years ago. It was *Tomarctus*, the ancestor of all the members of the dog family in the world today. It had very dog-like paws and ears, and may have hunted in packs. But it probably wasn't as smart as the dogs who came later.

The earliest members of the dog family began to develop about 7 or 8 million years ago. By about 300,000 years ago, animals that looked exactly like the wolves and jackals of today lived in Europe and Asia. Today the dog family, whose Latin name is *Canidae*, has about 35 different members. (We can only say "about," because scientists don't always agree on the way members of the family should be grouped.)

The *Canidae* are muscular hunters who can chase their prey for long distances. They kill it by snapping and slashing with their teeth. Most *Canidae* live in family groups at least part of the time, and many live in packs of 10 to 20 animals, or even more. People who study *Canidae* like to place them in smaller groupings of similar animals.

Each of these groupings is called a *genus*. For instance, many foxes are in *Genus Vulpes*. Wolves, jackals, coyotes, domestic dogs and dingoes, the wild dogs of Australia, are all in *Genus Canus*. Besides the pet dog (*Canis familiaris*), there are two members of *Genus Canis* in Canada: the wolf (*Canis lupus*) and the coyote (*Canis latrans*).

Wolves look a lot like German Shepherds or Huskies, but their legs are longer, their feet are larger, and their teeth are bigger and sharper. Their fur is usually a grey-brown mix, but it can also be white, black, or many different shades of brown. Wolves live in packs of up to 14 members, led by the biggest, strongest male. The animals have strong ties with each other. They take turns "baby-sitting" the young ones. When they go after larger animals such as deer, moose, and caribou, they hunt together. Since wolves aren't as strong or as fast as their prey, they have to outsmart them. Sometimes the pack splits up , and part of it will circle around to drive an animal towards the others who are lying in wait. Often the animal fights back or gets away. Wolves are only able to kill about one in 12 of the animals they track, and this is often an old or sick animal. Although wolves are rarely seen near built-up areas in the southern part of Canada, there is still a large wolf population farther north.

Swift Fox

Coyotes look like smaller greyish-brown wolves, but their muzzles are narrower and more pointed. We may think of coyotes as animals of the southwestern United States, but they are also found in Canada from Quebec to British Columbia. Coyotes live in family groups and hunt rabbits, mice, and ground squirrels. They will also eat *carrion* (dead meat) if they come upon it. Because they sometimes kill farm animals, they are hated and hunted by farmers and ranchers. However, the wily coyotes have managed to survive. In fact, they're found in more parts of North America now than they were 100 years ago.

Red Foxes (*Vulpes vulpes*) are found right across Canada, even on the outskirts of large cities. They have pointed faces and ears, silky fur, and thick, fluffy tails. These foxes hunt mostly at night and will eat almost anything: mice, squirrels, rabbits, berries, acorns, even grasshoppers. Canada has three other kinds of fox, but they are not as widespread. Arctic Foxes (see p. 31) live in the far North. Grey Foxes (*Urocyon cinereoargenteus*) are found only in southern Ontario and southern Manitoba. They live much like the Red Fox, except that they don't like to go as close to human settlements. Unlike most members of the dog family, Grey Foxes can climb trees, using their long, hooked claws.

Swift Foxes (*Vulpes velox*) are as small as housecats and can run more than 60 km/h (about 40 mph) . These foxes were once common on the Canadian Prairies, but too many of them were trapped for their thick pelts. By the 1930s, they had disappeared, although some survived in the United States. In the 1980s, the Canadian Wildlife Service set up a program to bring back the Swift Fox. Young foxes from Wyoming in the United States are being brought north and released. But it's still too soon to say whether the Swift Fox can make a comeback in its old home.

The Snow Fox

The Arctic Fox is the size of a large house cat, and its beautiful bushy tail makes up one-third of its length. Its thick white winter coat blends in with the snow, and its furred ears and feet stay warm even in the coldest weather. (In summer it wears a thinner mixed-brown coat.)

Although the Arctic Fox eats birds, eggs, berries, and fish (if it lives on the coast), its most important food is a little, fat rodent called a lemming. When there are lots of lemmings, there is plentiful food for the foxes. Fox families are large, usually about 11 pups. Fox parents have to catch more than 100 lemmings a day to feed their families. After a couple of years, though, there aren't enough lemmings left to feed the foxes. Then the foxes begin to starve, fewer babies are born, and their numbers go down. With fewer foxes to eat them, the lemming population grows again. Once more there are lots of lemmings for foxes to eat, more babies are born, and the whole cycle, which lasts about four years, starts again.

The Snow Fox (Alopex lagopus)
Home: the far north of North America, Europe and Asia
Weight: 2.5 to 9 kg (5.5 lbs. to almost 20 lbs.)
Food: lemmings; also ground squirrels, voles (small rodents) , fish, birds, eggs, berries, and the leftovers of wolf and polar bear kills

31

The Desert Fox

The Desert Fox, or Fennec, is the smallest wild member of the dog family. It has thick, cream-colored fur and a bushy tail with a white tip. The Fennec is well-suited to its desert home in North Africa and the Middle East. Air passing over the thin skin of the Fennec's huge ears carries away body heat, so the little fox stays cool. It can go for a long time without a drink of water. During the day, it burrows under the sand to get away from the heat of the sun. In the cooler evenings, the Fennec comes out to hunt insects, lizards, and small rodents. It has to watch out for the vultures, hyenas, and jackals that eat Fennecs. Usually its keen senses and speed help it outwit its enemies and get away. There is an Arab saying that "two dogs make a Fennec play, three dogs make him laugh, four make him run about, five make him flee, and six finally catch him."

The Fennec (Fennecus zerda)
Home: North Africa, and the Sinai and Arabian Peninsulas
Weight: about 1.5 kg (3 lbs.)
Food: lizards, snakes, rodents, and small birds; also scorpions, spiders, beetles, and other insects

A Dog's Life

You may have seen television shows about people who study wild animals such as gorillas or chimpanzees. These people spend years quietly watching the animals. They write down and photograph everything the animals do. If you are interested in learning more about how animals behave, you can start with an animal closer to home, your own dog. (If you don't have a pet, study a dog that belongs to a friend or relative.)

Things You'll Need:

a notebook and pencil

a camera

a watch with a second hand

1. Set aside 15 minutes every day to watch what your dog is doing. Don't always watch at the same time of day. Even if the dog is asleep, there are things to notice. How is the dog lying? Are its paws twitching? Does it make any sounds?
2. In your notebook, write what you see the dog doing. Put in as much detail as you can. Don't just write: "Sophie wanted to play." Write: "Sophie flattened her front half against the grass. Her front paws were stretched out. Her hindquarters were up in the air, and her tail was wagging fast. She barked twice — two short, sharp barks." You can take pictures of some of the things the dog does to back up your written report.
3. You might like to make a "time budget" for your dog. This will tell you how much time it spends on different

activities. You'll need a watch with a second hand. Watch the dog for a few minutes. Every 30 seconds, write down what the dog is doing at that instant. If the dog is being very active, you might like to write something every 15 seconds. (Just make quick notes and write them out in fuller form later.)

Here's a time budget that Rick made for Dana, his Shetland Sheepdog.

	Minutes and Seconds
0:00	Dana is in the kitchen, drinking from her water dish with a loud lapping sound.
0:30	She is still drinking.
1:00	She is walking into the living room, nuzzling her chew stick toy as she passes it.
1:30	Dana is lying down on the living room rug, resting her head on her right front paw.
2:00	She is still lying down, but has moved her head to her left front paw.
2:30	Dana is sitting up, using her right rear foot to scratch the right side of her head.
3:00	She is lying down again, with her head resting on the rug between her paws.
3:30	Dana is still lying down in the same position, with her eyes closed. She looks like she's sleeping.

4. After you've watched your dog closely for a week or so, you can figure out which things it does often and which things it does rarely. Think about your pet's activities. Why do you think your dog acts the way it does?
5. You can take out your notebook again after a few weeks, months, or even years, and see whether your dog's behavior is different. (If you have a puppy to watch, it would be very interesting to record how its activities change as it gets older.)

Family Ties

A friend's dog has had puppies and you're trying to choose one for your pet. Five eager little faces look up at you. At first they look exactly the same. Then you notice that one seems a little bigger and stronger than the others. One has a pink nose like its father and the others have black noses like their mother. Although they look quite a bit like each other, and quite a bit like their parents, each puppy is *unique* (different from the others).

Why is it that when dogs have puppies, the puppies look like their parents? (Poodles always have baby Poodles, not baby Great Danes.) Yet why is it that each puppy is something new, not exactly like either parent or exactly like its brothers and sisters? The answer lies in the way that dogs and other animals *reproduce* (make more of themselves).

When a male and a female animal mate, each one gives a little of itself to make its *offspring* (babies). That is why puppies look similar to their parents. Each new puppy starts with an egg cell from its mother and a sperm cell from its father. The egg cell and the sperm cell each contain *half* of the instructions to make a puppy. The puppy is a new mixture of features that have never been put together before. And that is why a puppy doesn't look *exactly* like either of its parents.

When the egg and sperm cells join together, they make a *zygote* (sometimes called a fertilized egg) that can divide into more and more cells until a new puppy is formed. The zygote has complete instructions, half from mother, half from father, for what the puppy will look like and how it will grow. These instructions are called *genes*. There are genes in every cell of your dog's body — and yours, too. Both of you have thousands and thousands of genes.

Single genes are far too tiny for anyone to see. However, they are carried on little thread-like structures that we *can* see under a microscope. These threads are called *chromosomes*. You can think of genes as little beads on these threads. Every kind of animal has its own special genes and chromosomes, which the parents pass on to their children. You, and every other human being, have 23 pairs of chromosomes. Your dog — let's call him Cody — has 39 pairs.

One chromosome in each pair came from Cody's mother and one in each pair came from his father. On each pair of chromosomes, the genes are also lined up in matched pairs, like two strings of identical beads. For instance, one pair of genes might decide the color of Cody's coat. Suppose he got a gene for a black coat (we'll label it B) from his mother and a gene for a black coat (B) from his father. Cody's coat would be black, too. However, suppose he got a gene for a black coat (B) from his mother and a gene for a white coat (b) from his father. What would happen then?

The whole set of genes that a baby animal inherits from its parents is called its *genotype*. But not all of these genes can express themselves. For instance, you can have blue eyes like your father *or* brown eyes like your mother, but not both. Cody can have a black coat like his mother or a white coat like his father. Which will it be? Some genes are stronger at expressing themselves than others. These are called *dominant* genes.

Dominant genes always show themselves, no matter what the other gene for the same feature says. So if Cody gets BB from his two parents, he will be black. If he gets Bb, he will *still* be black, because the black coat color gene is stronger than the white one. *Only* if Cody gets a gene for a white coat (bb) from both parents can he be white. The weaker gene for a white coat is called a *recessive* gene. Recessive genes only show themselves when you, or your dog, inherit them from *both* parents.

We can't see Cody's complete genotype. We can only see his *phenotype* (all the genes that actually express themselves). However, by looking at his parents and his brothers and sisters, we can figure out what genes for coat color he is carrying, both the one that shows and the one that doesn't show. Suppose that Cody's mother has a black coat (BB) and his father has a white coat (bb). What will their puppies look like? Here's a simple chart to show you:

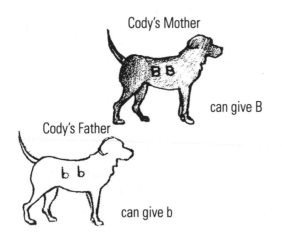

Cody's Mother

can give B

Cody's Father

can give b

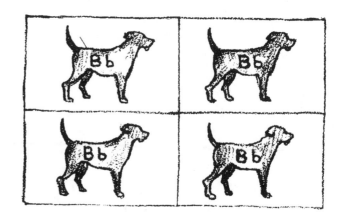

All the puppies, including Cody, will have black coats like their mother, even though all of them are carrying a recessive white gene from their father, too. (They are all Bb.) Now suppose that Cody grows up and mates with another dog, Cleo, who is also Bb. What will their puppies look like? The chart at the bottom of the page shows you.

People who study the actions of genes have found this pattern over and over again. If both parents are carrying the dominant and recessive genes for some feature, the odds are three in four that their children will show the dominant feature.

The odds are only one in four that a child will show the recessive feature. In the case of Cody's and Cleo's puppies, one is "pure" black coat, two have black coats but can still pass the gene for white coat to their children, and one is "pure" white coat.

When you consider that dogs — and people — have *thousands* of genes to pass on to their children in various combinations, you can start to see why brothers and sisters aren't exactly alike, even though they have the same parents. In the whole history of the world, there has only ever been, and there will only ever be, one Cody. And one you!

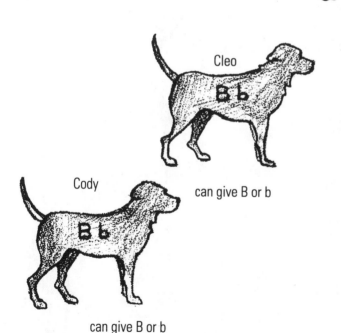

Cleo
Bb

Cody
Bb

can give B or b

can give B or b

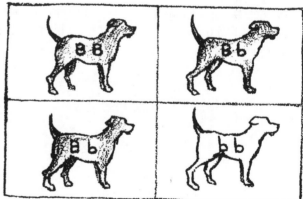

Bow-WOW!

Who are the biggest members of the dog family? The answer depends on how you look at it. The Old English Mastiff and the St. Bernard are the heaviest dog breeds. Full-grown males of these breeds often weigh 91 kg (200 lbs.). An Old English Mastiff named Alcama Zorba of La-Susa weighs in at 144.66 kg (319 lbs.). Alcama Zorba is not overweight, he's just massive! He also holds the record as the world's longest dog, 254.4 cm (100 ins.).

Great Danes and Irish Wolfhounds don't hold any weight records, but they're the world's tallest dogs. They're often more than 99 cm (39 ins.) high at the shoulder, which is how dog height is measured. This means they can look straight into the eyes of the average six year old. Standing on their hind legs, they can easily put their paws on the chests of people who are over 183 cm (6 ft.) tall, and look down on them! The tallest dog on record was a Great Dane named Shamgret Danzas, who died in 1984. He stood a towering 105.4 cm (41-1/2 ins.) at the shoulder. (Heavyweight champ Alcama Zorba measures only 88.7 cm (35 ins.).

Irish
Wolfhound

Fishing In the Gene Pool

Things You'll Need:

a plain sheet of paper

6 green index cards and 6 yellow index cards (or any other two colors)

a few facts about human genes:

1. Human beings have 23 pairs of chromosomes. Each chromosome in a pair carries genes for the same features. But the genes themselves may not be the same. One chromosome may have a gene for dark hair (D) and the other may have a gene for light-colored hair (d). Researchers have found out that dark hair (D) is *dominant* (stronger), while light hair (d) is *recessive* (weaker). (For more about this, read pages 35 to 37.) So someone who carries Dd genes still has dark hair. Only someone who carries dd will actually have light-colored hair.
2. Every baby gets half its chromosomes from its mother and half from its father. Since parents' chromosomes also come in pairs, it's up to chance which half of each pair the baby will get.

What to do:

1. Use six green cards for Mom's chromosomes. To keep things simple, we'll pretend she only has three pairs of chromosomes. To make things even simpler, we'll pretend she only has one gene on each chromosome.

Label the cards like this:

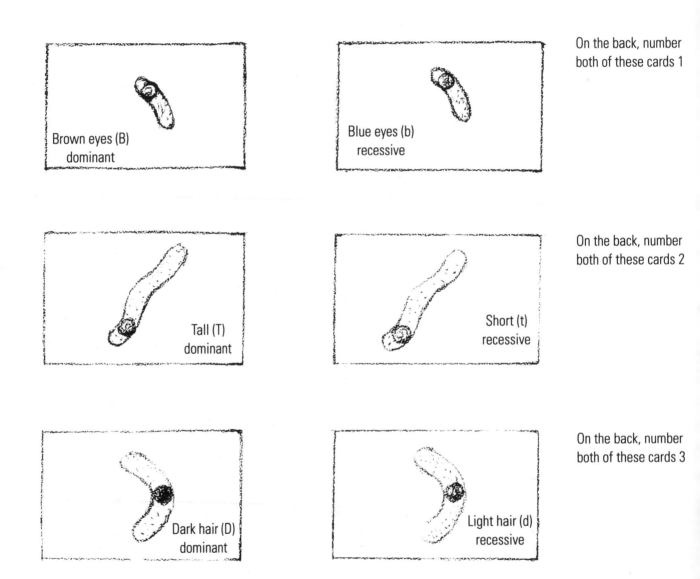

Brown eyes (B)
dominant

Blue eyes (b)
recessive

On the back, number
both of these cards 1

Tall (T)
dominant

Short (t)
recessive

On the back, number
both of these cards 2

Dark hair (D)
dominant

Light hair (d)
recessive

On the back, number
both of these cards 3

40

2. Use six yellow cards for Dad's chromosomes. Make them match Mom's cards.

3. Lay out Mom's cards, face down, keeping the chromosome pairs side by side. Lay out Dad's cards face down, with the chromosome pairs side by side. Now you have a "gene pool." To make new chromosome pairs for a child, take one of each pair from Mom and one of each pair from Dad, so that the child also has three pairs. Turn them over. What genes does the child have? What does the child look like? (Remember, if the child has one dominant gene and one recessive gene, only the dominant one will show.)

4. Try this a few times. How many different combinations can you make? Keep track with a chart like this:

	Height genes	Eye-color genes	Hair-color genes	Appearance
Child 1	TT	Bb	dd	Tall, brown eyes, light hair
Child 2	tt	bb	Dd	Short, blue eyes, dark hair

How many blue-eyed children do you get? How many brown-eyed? How many tall children compared with how many short ones? How many dark-haired children compared with light-haired?

Are you surprised at all the combinations you can get with just three pairs of chromosomes? Imagine how many combinations you would get with 23 pairs of chromosomes and thousands of genes! That's why each new baby will never be exactly like its older brothers and sisters.

Dogs Up Close

All Shapes and Sizes

Dogs come in an amazing range of shapes and sizes. A Saint Bernard can easily be 300 times the weight of a tiny Yorkshire Terrier. A Great Dane may be 10 times the height of a Yorkie. Can you imagine what it would be like if people varied this much? There would be women who weighed 50 kg (110 lbs.) and women who weighed 15,000 kg (33,000 lbs.). That's heavier than an elephant! There would be men who were 170 cm (5 ft., 6 ins.) tall and men who were 1700 cm (56 ft.) tall. That's more than twice as tall as a giraffe!

Dogs come in yellow and white and black and gray and every shade of brown. There are even *brindled* (striped) dogs such as Boxers, and spotted breeds such as Dalmatians and English Setters. Labrador Retrievers, who are strong swimmers, have smooth, waterproof coats. Siberian Huskies and other hardy northern dogs have thick, two-layered coats to keep out wintry blasts. Komodors and Pulis have strange-looking coats made of long woolly cords, while Mexican Hairless dogs have no fur at all, except for a few wisps on their heads and tails.

Dogs' skulls can be long and pointed like a Collie's, wide and flat like a Pekingese's, or somewhere in between. Their ears may point up like a German Shepherd's, fold over in a soft flap like an Irish Terrier's, or flop loosely beside their heads like a Bloodhound's or an Afghan's.

No other animal has as many different body shapes as dogs do. Still, when we see a small dog such as a Maltese, we know it's not a cat. When we see a huge dog like an Irish Wolfhound, we know it's not a pony. What are some of the things that all dogs have in common?

No matter how different the shape of their heads, all adult dogs have 42 teeth. (Adult human beings have 32.)

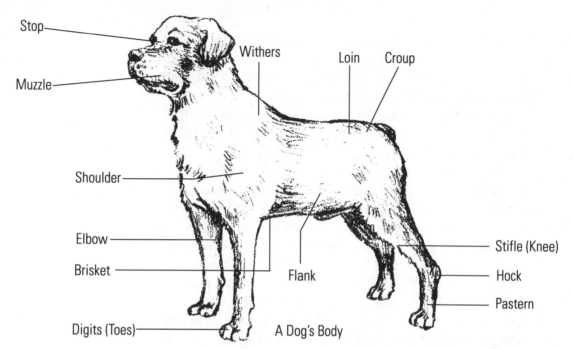

Stop

Muzzle

Withers

Loin

Croup

Shoulder

Elbow

Brisket

Flank

Stifle (Knee)

Hock

Pastern

Digits (Toes)

A Dog's Body

At the front of their mouths, top and bottom, are six small chisel-shaped teeth for nibbling. Beside these are long sharp fangs, one on each side, top and bottom. These are for killing prey and tearing at meat. Behind them, on each side, are eight shearing teeth (four uppers and four lowers) that meet like scissor blades.

Finally, dogs have five heavy grinding teeth at the back of their mouths. There are five on each side, two uppers and three lowers. These flat molars can crunch bones and also mash up leaves and grains. Although dogs are usually classed as *carnivores* because they eat meat, they can also be called *omnivores* (everything-eaters). Like human beings, and unlike cats, dogs have a mixture of "meat-eating" and plant-eating teeth.

All dogs have the same basic framework of bones and muscles. Like their wolf ancestors, dogs are built for running. Lean, long-legged Greyhounds can run up to 70 km/h (over

40 mph) , but most dogs are not sprinters. They're long-distance runners. A dog's heart is much bigger for the size of its body than yours. It pumps oxygen-rich blood to the dog's leg muscles so they don't get achy and tired.

Walking animals, such as bears, step on the soles of their feet. Running animals, such as dogs and cats, walk on their toes. That sharp bend in a dog's hind leg is actually its heelbone. A dog has four toes on each hind foot and five toes on each front foot. The fifth toe, called a dew claw, is small and useless. A dog's claws are strong enough to grip the ground, but not long enough to catch and slow it down. Because a dog can't pull in its claws like a cat, the tips get too blunt to use for climbing trees or clawing enemies.

A dog's paw is cushioned with fleshy pads. These pads are the only part of a dog's body that can sweat. The liquid keeps the dog's feet from cracking and drying out. The dog also leaves behind a sweaty trail that other dogs can smell.

You have sweat glands all over your body. When sweat *evaporates* (goes into the air) from your skin, it carries heat away. But small sweating footpads aren't enough to cool a dog. Instead, a hot dog cools off by panting. The dog breathes in through its nose and out through its mouth, up to 300 times a minute. The rushing air helps to evaporate water from the inside surface of the dog's breathing passages, mouth and tongue. As the liquid evaporates, it carries heat away from the dog's body.

SURPRISING FACTS ABOUT DOGS

Hot Digitty Dog

In the early 1900s, a man named Harry Stevens thought of a new kind of snack food to sell at New York baseball games. He tucked German sausages (the kind we call wieners or frankfurters) inside bread rolls. People could pass these wrapped sausages through the stands without getting their hands messy, and they were a big hit.

The sausages reminded Ted Dorgan, a sports cartoonist, of Dachshund dogs. Both were long, thin, reddish-brown and came from Germany. He drew a cartoon of a Dachshund yapping inside a bread roll. Dorgan wasn't sure how to spell the dog's name, so he just labeled his drawing "Hot Dog." The cartoon became very popular and soon everyone was calling the new snack a hotdog.

SOMETHING TO SEND FOR

WHAT'S FLYBALL?

Flyball is a fast exciting sport for dogs and people. Relay teams of four dogs compete against each other. Two dogs from opposing teams race side by side down the flyball course. Each dog goes over four jumps, steps on a box pedal to release a tennis ball, then races back over the jumps with the tennis ball in its mouth. In the meantime, the human spectators are clapping, hollering, and jumping up and down as they cheer their favorites. Dogs of many different breeds—and mixed-breed dogs too—can enjoy flyball. Do you think you and your dog would like to give it a try? You can send for some free brochures that tell you all about flyball and the North American Flyball Association.

Write to:
Mr. Mike Randall, President
North American Flyball Association
1342 Jeff Street
Ypsilanti, Michigan
U.S.A. 48198

Ask for: Flyball brochures

Don't Forget: Print your own address clearly on your letter, so Mr. Randall will know where to send your booklet.

Super, Natural Senses

One summer afternoon, Carla the German Shepherd is walking peacefully across a field with her owner, Susan. Then Carla stops so suddenly that Susan almost falls over her. Susan looks around and sees nothing. She tugs on Carla's leash, but Carla refuses to move. The hair rises on Carla's shoulders and back. She growls menacingly at the empty path in front of her. After a couple of minutes, Carla returns to her walk as if nothing has happened. But Susan keeps thinking about her dog's strange behavior. Did Carla see a ghost?

Clancy, a mixed-breed terrier, suddenly leaps up from his mat and runs to the door. He wags his tail happily. The other members of the Goodman family look up and smile. "Dad must be on his way," they say. No one else in the family can hear anyone approaching. Yet, sure enough, five minutes later, David Goodman arrives home from work.

Dogs do things like this fairly often, so it's no wonder some people believe that their dogs have a "sixth sense" that can't be explained. They don't realize a dog's normal senses are so keen that they seem supernatural to us. Carla was probably stopped in her tracks by something she smelled, not by something she saw. She may have smelled a fox or a raccoon that was several hundred meters away. (For more about a dog's sense of smell, see p. 52). Clancy was likely reacting to sounds too faint for people to hear.

Dogs can hear sounds from distances four times farther away than a human being can. A dog can hear a sound from the end of the block that you could only hear if it were in the next room. When dogs listen, they "prick up their ears" so that their ear flaps can gather the sounds efficiently. Although dogs with ears that stand up hear best, even flop-eared dogs hear far better than people.

Sounds are made by something that is *vibrating* (shaking back and forth very fast.) These vibrations make the air around the thing vibrate, too. When vibrations hit dogs' ears (and yours) they hear a sound. The faster a thing vibrates, the higher the sound it makes. We use *Herz* to measure how fast a sound wave vibrates. A dog can hear sounds from about 20 or 30 Hz, which is a very low rumble, to over 40,000 Hz. In fact, some researchers think a dog can hear as high as 100,000 Hz, the high squeak of a bat. Although you can hear the same low sounds as a dog, you can't hear much above 20,000 Hz . (When you're an adult, your ears will be even less sensitive to high-pitched sounds.) Dogs must sometimes wonder why people don't react when someone whistles two streets away, or mice squeak in the attic!

In one important way, though, your world is more vivid than your dog's. People who study dogs believe that they don't see colors very well. They probably see green and red as shades of gray and other colors likely look pale. Dogs' eyes aren't as good as yours at seeing the fine detail of things, either.

A dog's eye, like yours, works by taking in the light that reflects off objects. The light goes into the eye through the black opening called the *pupil*. Just behind the pupil is a *lens*. The lens bends the light coming into the eye so that it can *focus* (form a clear image) on the back of the eye. A dog's lens isn't as good at bending light as yours is, so things look fuzzier. A dog can't see someone standing about 270 m (300 yds.) away, if the person keeps still. However, if the person moves even a little, the dog will likely notice the motion. In fact, shepherds working with sheepdogs can wave a command to their dogs from more than a kilometer away.

Hunting dogs that are famous for their eyesight, such as Greyhounds, probably don't see details better than any other dog. However, their heads are long and narrow, and their eyes are set well back. This means they have a sweeping view to both sides without even turning their heads. Even flat-faced dogs whose eyes face front have a wider view than you do. There's a price to pay for this broad sweep, though. Dogs can't judge distance as well as you can.

The greater the sweep of a dog's vision, the less overlap there is in what its two eyes are seeing. But you need this overlap to judge how far away something is. To prove this to yourself, try closing one eye and bringing the tips of your index fingers together. It's easy with two eyes, but tricky with just one.

There is one way in which dogs' eyes work better than yours. They can see more clearly in dim light. They have an extra layer, called the *tapetum*, at the back of their eyes. When light comes into dogs' eyes, the tapetum acts like a mirror to bounce some of it back. This means that dogs' eyes, unlike yours, have another chance to use every last bit of light.

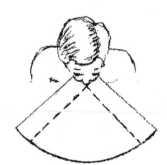 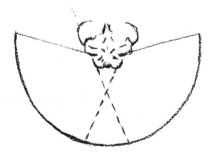 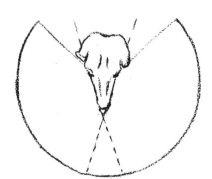

Lights, Camera, Action!

Dog actors have been making people laugh and cry for a long time. Shakespeare wrote a walk-on part for a dog in *Two Gentlemen of Verona* in 1591. More than three hundred years later, a German Shepherd named Rin Tin Tin was one of the biggest stars in the movies. An American soldier found him on a battlefield in Europe during World War I. Rinty carried messages for the Red Cross and became a war hero. After the war, his owner trained him for the movies. Soon the dog was earning $2,000 a week, at a time when few people earned that much in a year.

Lassie was the next canine superstar. The collie was in seven movies between 1943 and 1951. Lassie was a star with a secret. "She" was really a laddie named Pal. (The trainer said that male collies had better coats.) Although Lassie was a talented performer, he sometimes had special help. For a big homecoming scene in *Lassie Come Home*, a child's face was smeared with ice cream to make sure Lassie gave him adoring licks! Lassie's sons and grandsons starred in a popular *Lassie* TV series that ran for 19 years.

Benji has been the biggest dog star of recent years. The little shaggy mixed-breed female started her acting career when she was only eleven months old. (She inherited the job from her father, also named Benji, who had starred in a TV series.) By 1990, her movies, TV specials, and personal appearances had earned over $100 million dollars!

Benji

Scent-Sational Skills

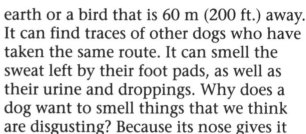

On a cold December night in 1988, a German Shepherd named Daisy was picking her way over the rubble of a collapsed apartment building. Suddenly she pawed at the ground and began to dig frantically. Daisy had scented human beings trapped under tons of concrete! A few hours later, rescuers were able to pull these people out. They were still alive, thanks to Daisy and her handler, Bill Grimer.

Daisy and Bill were far from their New Brunswick home that night. They were one of 250 SAR (Search And Rescue) teams who had come to Soviet Armenia from all over the world. A powerful earthquake had flattened whole cities and buried thousands of people. The human rescuers didn't know where to dig first. They needed dogs, with their powerful sense of smell, to show them.

Every day, somewhere in the world, people are putting dogs' noses to work. Police forces use dogs who are specially trained to sniff out hidden bombs and illegal drugs. Tracking dogs follow scent trails to find lost children and escaped criminals. Dogs like Daisy find people under fallen buildings or under deep snow after an avalanche.

Your dog's nose works so well that it can smell a bone under 60 cm (24 ins.) of earth or a bird that is 60 m (200 ft.) away. It can find traces of other dogs who have taken the same route. It can smell the sweat left by their foot pads, as well as their urine and droppings. Why does a dog want to smell things that we think are disgusting? Because its nose gives it so much interesting news about other dogs. Your dog can tell whether they were males or females, adults or puppies, friends or strangers. Your dog can even figure out how these dogs were feeling, since fear or anger change the smells they leave behind. If your dog smells "dog fear," for instance, it might mean there's some danger nearby.

You and your dog smell things in much the same way. How does the sense of smell work? And why can your dog smell things much better than you can?

The part of your nose that smells things is only about the size of a postage stamp. This little patch, high up inside your nose, is called the *olfactory membrane*. It contains millions of very tiny nerve cells with little hair-like things called *cilia* sticking out of them. The whole membrane patch is covered with a liquid called *mucous*.

You can only smell something when you breathe in tiny bits of it. The bits are caught on the little cilia and dissolve in the mucous. These tiny bits are *molecules*, the building blocks of everything in the world. Some of the molecules in a thing may break off and float through the air. Then you can sniff them up your nose.

Like you, your dog has an olfactory membrane inside its nose, but it's much bigger than yours. Laid out flat, it would cover the area of about 50 postage stamps. You have about 5 million nerve cells in your nose; a dog has about 220 million. This means that a dog can smell a much fainter whiff of something than you can. In fact, a dog's sense of smell for butyric acid, a chemical found in sweat, is a *million* times better than yours.

What happens in your nose, and your dog's, is only part of the story on smells. All of your senses need your nerves and your brain to work properly. Nerves, acting like telephone wires, carry smell messages from the special cells in your nose up to your brain. Your brain sorts out the messages and decides what they mean. It may even decide not to pay any attention to them! Unless an odor is strong or unusual or you're making a special effort to sniff something, you often don't notice smells.

Something strange happens even when you're paying special attention to an odor. Have you ever come into the house and smelled muffins baking? Mmmmmm! But after you've been home a few minutes,

you can't smell the muffins anymore. The nerve cells in your nose have stopped sending muffin messages to your brain. This is called *olfactory fatigue*.

Long ago, wild members of the dog family used their sense of smell to hunt food, find mates, and keep away from their enemies. It's still a dog's most important sense. The area that receives smell messages takes up a bigger portion of a dog's brain than it does of yours, so these messages get lots of attention. Furthermore, a dog who is tracking a scent needs to be able to keep smelling it. It can cure its olfactory fatigue by taking short, sharp sniffs of air.

Some dogs have a keener sense of smell than others. Slow-moving bloodhounds, with their saggy jowls and long, floppy ears, are amazingly good at following the trail of human beings. In 1983, three ten-year-old girls got lost while they were on a camping trip in a Connecticut state park. Searchers looked for them all through the night, while their parents waited anxiously. In the morning, an old bloodhound named Clem joined the search. He was given a piece of clothing that belonged to one of the girls to sniff. Then Clem set off, pulling hard on his leash. After 2 km (1-1/4 miles), he found a purple hairclip that one of the girls had dropped. Clem plodded on, his nose to the ground, until he came to a swamp. When the searchers shouted, they got a reply! The girls were on the other side of the swamp, wet and exhausted. Once they were safely home, the girls sent Clem a present.

It's odd to think that your dog lives in a rich world of smells that you can never enter. But many human beings owe their lives to dogs' scent-sational skills.

Nifty Sniff Tests

How keen is your dog's sense of smell?

1. Meat Feat

Things You'll Need:

4 or 5 sheets of newspaper

a small piece of meat

3 or 4 other small things, but not food

1. Wrap the piece of meat in a sheet of newspaper. Wash your hands so that you don't put the meat smell on anything else. Then wrap the other small things in newspaper too, so that all the packages look the same.
2. Spread the packages on the floor. Now bring in your dog. Give the dog a chance to sniff the packages. How long does it take your dog to find the meat?

2. Find the Ball

Things You'll Need:

a rubber ball

1. Rub the ball with your hands to put your scent all over it.
2. Give your dog a chance to sniff the ball.
3. Put your dog where it can't see what you do next.
4. Walk to a spot where you'll hide the ball, perhaps behind a bush or tree. (Pick a spot only a couple of meters away for your dog's first tracking effort.) Drag your feet heavily

on the ground to make sure you leave a scent trail. Hide the ball.

5. Bring your pet to the beginning of the scent trail you laid down and point it in the right direction. Can your dog find the ball?

How To Speak Dog

It's not hard to tell when Sunshine, the Labrador Retriever, wants to play. The front part of her body is crouching. Her hindquarters are up in the air, and her tail is wagging frantically. Most people can understand a doggie "bow" right away.

People usually *communicate* (tell each other their thoughts and feelings) by using their voices. Dogs "speak" too, with growls and whines and barks. But dogs also send a lot of messages with their ears, their tails, and even the way they stand. This is called *body language*.

Long ago, dogs' wolf ancestors lived and hunted in packs. This is the way wolves still live today. The pack members have to be able to settle their arguments, warn each other of danger, and make decisions. Wolves who want to be leader need a way to show the others they are big and strong. Weaker wolves need ways to behave so that the others will not attack them. A lot of dog talk comes from their ancient days as wild hunters. But, as you'll see, some of it comes from living with people.

In the wild, young wolves whine to show that they're cold or hungry. Adult wolves don't use the sound much. But pet dogs stay puppy-like with their human families even when they are grown up. They whine when they're unhappy. Sometimes they even whimper in sympathy when their person looks upset. A whine means "I need company," but a growl means just the opposite: "I'm warning you, stay away."

Dogs bark much more than wolves do. When wolves bark, they're usually sounding an alarm. Ancient people may have chosen and bred dogs who barked, because the animals would give them early warning of an attack. Today, people often wish dogs would bark less! They bark when they're alone, if they're bored or lonely. They bark to defend their homes against strangers. They bark when they're excited. Barks can mean many things and people can often understand their own dog's different kinds of barks. But to understand dogs really well, you also have to look at their body language.

How does a dog look when it wants to be *dominant* ("top dog")? It stands boldly with its tail held up and its ears standing up straight. It's trying to look as big and strong as it can. A top dog that's thinking about fighting carries this even further. It raises the hair on its back to make itself look even bigger. It stares at its enemy. It wrinkles its nose and raises its lip to show its sharp teeth.

A dog that wants to say, "I know you're top dog, let's be friends" tries to look as small and harmless as it can. (This is called being *submissive*.) A submissive dog crouches, flattens its ears, and lowers its tail. It may even roll over on its back. Most dogs treat their people as leaders of the pack, so they often act submissive toward them. When dogs are afraid, they may look submissive and angry at the same time. They lay their ears back and hold their bodies low, but they growl and may even attack.

As you can see, dogs' ears and tails send important messages. In fact, some of the changes people have made to dogs' bodies make it harder for dogs to talk. Dog breeds with floppy ears look submissive to other dogs, whether they feel that way or not. Dog breeds that have no tails to wag often wiggle their whole hindquarters instead.

While dog owners are trying hard to understand their dogs, dogs are working hard at learning human language. Dogs know their names and commands such as "Sit" and "Stay." Most dogs can pick words that are important to them, such as "walk" or "dinner," out of sentences. Dogs are also very skilled at reading human body language. For instance, Sunshine waits for a signal that it's time for her evening walk. Her 12-year-old owner, Josh, hasn't moved from his chair yet. But she notices him tense his muscles just before he gets up. And Sunshine, seeming to be a mind reader, bounds joyfully to the front door.

Some dogs have even learned a goofy, toothy smile from watching human faces. This smile is only for their favorite people, never for another dog!

Going Through the Motions

Brandy the Irish Setter had eaten a big dinner. Her tummy was full, but her dish still had some dog food in it. She sniffed the dish and began to nudge it with her nose. Soon Brandy had pushed her dish to the far corner of the room. Why did she do that?

Maxim the Boxer was ready for his nap. He walked over to his blanket in the corner of the family room. Before he settled down, he turned himself in circles—once, twice, three times. Finally, with a contented sigh, he settled down on his blanket. Why did he turn in circles before going to sleep?

Dogs have lived with people in their houses for more than 10,000 years. But they still share many habits with wild members of the dog family, including their wolf ancestors. Wolves hunt in packs when they kill a large animal such as a deer. They bolt down as much of the meat as they can. If there are some good meaty bones left over, the wolves bury them for later. They dig a hole with their front paws, drop the meat in, and push the dirt over it with their noses. Brandy had no bone to bury, but she had some leftovers she couldn't eat. So she used her nose to "bury" the whole food dish in the corner of the room. If she does this a lot, it's a message to her family that they're overfeeding her.

When wild dogs want to sleep, they trample a smooth spot in the tall grass so they'll have a comfortable, hidden place to lie down. Even though Maxim really didn't need to flatten his napping place, he still went through the motions that worked for his wolf ancestors.

Don't Get Bitten!

Sometimes an unlucky person meets a dangerous dog, perhaps one that has been bred or trained to attack. But this is rare. Usually when people are chased or bitten by a dog, it's because they didn't know a few simple safety rules.

If you see a dog walking with its owner, always *ask first* if you may pet the dog. Even if the owner says yes, don't rush up to the dog or suddenly hug it. Look at it first. Is it wagging its tail? Does it seem relaxed and friendly? If it does, stretch out your hand so the dog can sniff it. After that, you can pat or scratch the dog gently. What if the dog backs away, growls, or looks tense? Then, no matter what the owner said, forget about petting it. The dog is not ready to be friends with you.

Never tease a dog that is penned up or chained on its own property. For one thing, it's cruel to torment the animal. Also, the dog might break loose and come after you.

Sometimes children are bitten by their own pets. Even a dog that is usually good-natured can snap if it's angry or frightened. Never try to take a toy or food away from a dog. Never grab or startle a sleeping dog.

What do you do if you're outside and you meet an unfriendly dog? Suppose it's barking and growling at you or snarling with its teeth showing, and there's no one around to help? DON'T RUN. If you do, the dog will probably chase you and may snap at your heels. Back slowly away from the dog. Don't look the dog in the eyes, because it may take this as a challenge. Say "Go home!" in a loud, stern voice. The dog likely won't follow you for more than a few steps.

Pooches In Proverbs

Bernard of Clairvaux, a French religious leader in the twelfth century, was famous for his learning and good works. He is also famous for saying, "Who loves me will love my dog also," or as we put it today, "Love me, love my dog." In Spain, they say "Do you want a dog to love you? Feed it!" A Turkish proverb says, "If a dog's prayers were answered, bones would rain from the sky." There are lots of sayings in English that refer to dogs. How many of these do you know?

You can't teach an old dog new tricks.
Let sleeping dogs lie.
His bark is worse than his bite.
Don't go barking up the wrong tree.
Every dog has his day.
The tail is wagging the dog.

Taking Care Of Your Dog

The Right Dog For You

Which dog is right for you and your family? A romping Golden Retriever? A gentle giant Newfoundland? A playful little Dachshund? There are hundreds of different dog breeds in the world. There are also mixed-breed dogs ("mutts") of every shape, size, and color.

Animal shelter cages are full of sad-eyed dogs who "didn't work out." Their families gave them up because they were too noisy or active, or they grew too big, or they shed hairs all over the furniture. Too often, people pick out a cute puppy without finding out how big it will grow, how thick a coat it will have, or how much exercise it will need.

Some of the very large dogs, such as Newfoundlands, are gentle and make good family pets. However, they have appetites to match their size. They also need lots of room. If your family is living in a small home or on a tight budget, these dogs aren't a good choice. Some very small dogs are too nervous and delicate to play with children. However, some toy breeds, such as the English Toy Spaniel, are hardy enough to be part of a noisy, active family .

Samoyeds and Old English Sheepdogs have thick coats that need lots of brushing and trimming. Is someone in your family willing to do the work? Is there money in the family budget to take the dog to a groomer? Other dogs, such as Beagles, have coats that need very little care. Some breeds, including Irish Setters and Golden Retrievers, need to run every day. Is there an open space near your home where your dog can get the exercise it needs? Are you willing to take the dog out for long walks, even when it's raining?

You can find out about dog breeds from library books and by talking to friends and relatives who already own a dog. If you can, go to a dog show. You'll be surprised at all the different kinds of dogs on display. If a dog catches your interest, ask its owner what the breed is like and what special care it needs. You and your family can make an appointment to go and see a breeder's dogs at their home kennel. You can also read dog magazines to find out about dog breeders and their dogs.

A purebred or pedigreed puppy has had its whole family tree planned by human breeders. A few breeders try so hard to breed good-looking dogs who will win prizes at dog shows that they don't pay enough attention to other qualities. They may produce puppies who are nervous and sickly and wouldn't make good pets. Sometimes people become dog breeders just to make money. Instead of trying to produce the best dogs they can, they simply try to produce as many as they can.

Fortunately, most breeders aren't like this. If you find a breeder who has been raising one kind of dog for many years, who won't sell you a puppy without finding out all about how you will care for it, and who offers to take the puppy back if you are unhappy with it, you've likely found a good breeder. Often this person will give you a chance to see a puppy's parents and even its grandparents. If they are good-tempered, healthy dogs, your puppy will probably be the same. And you can see what the puppy will look like when it grows up.

If you get to see all the puppies in a litter, you'll notice that they don't all behave the same way. One of them may be very loud, barking and growling at you. That puppy may be hard to train. Another one may back into the corner, trembling. That puppy may be too nervous to make a good family pet. Choose the pup that seems confident and interested in you. The ideal age to take a puppy home is when it is between six and eight weeks old.

Purebred puppies cost hundreds of dollars, and many people just can't afford them. However, you can also find a good family pet, for much less money, at your local animal shelter. You may even get a purebred dog that has been lost or given away by its family—although it will probably be an adult or a "teenager" (eight to twelve months old). People are sometimes worried about getting an animal from a shelter. They've heard stories of cute little puppies who grew into giant-sized dogs. Or they're afraid that an adult dog will be badly behaved. After all, someone already got rid of it. But the staff at an animal shelter can help you make a good choice. For instance, they can judge by a puppy's size (especially by the size of its paws) how big it is likely to grow. They'll help you find a dog that is right for your family.

If you take the time to choose carefully, your dog will be an enjoyable and much-loved member of your family for as long as it lives.

SOMETHING TO SEND FOR

A Dog's Best Friend. . .

A dog's best friend is the person who takes good care of it. Do you know how to choose the right toy for your dog? Do you know which human food treats should not be given to dogs? Do you know how to tell when your dog needs to see a veterinarian right away? The Toronto Humane Society's *Handbook of Dog Care* is a 30-page guide to keeping your pet in top condition.

Write to:
Toronto Humane Society
11 River Street
Toronto, Ontario
M5A 4C2

Ask for: Handbook of Dog Care

Cost: $1.50

Don't forget: Print your own address clearly on your letter, so that the Humane Society will know where to send your booklet.

Pooch Scoop

Dog droppings spoil the look of your neighborhood and they can also spread germs. In some communities, it's against the law to let your dog make a mess unless you clean it up right away. It's easy to make a pooch scoop that you can take with you when you're walking your dog. Scoop the wastes into a bag, carry them home, and flush them down the toilet.

Things You'll Need:
1.5 to 2 L (48 to 70 fl. oz.) plastic bottle with a handle on the side

marker that can write on plastic

scissors

1. Turn the bottle on its side, with the handle facing up. Draw a scoop shape on the plastic, as shown in the drawing. This will be your guideline for cutting
2. Ask an adult to start the cutting by puncturing the plastic with a knife. Then you can use scissors to cut along the line. Now you've got a handy pooch scoop to take along when you walk your dog.

This is a good way to recycle plastic containers. You can use the scoops for gardening, or as sandbox toys. Make extras for gifts or to take to the beach.

Welcome Home

At the end of the week, you'll be bringing a new puppy home. Is your family ready for the newcomer? The first thing to do is to "puppyproof" your home. Like human babies, puppies explore their world by putting things in their mouths. Make sure electrical cords are out of the puppy's reach so that it can't chew on them. Put household chemicals like soaps and cleansers into a cupboard your pet can't get into. Many house plants are poisonous to pets, so put them on high shelves.

You should think about a name for your pet. A dog will learn a short, simple name more quickly than a long one. (Even purebred dogs, who often have long, fancy names that show their family history, have shorter names for everyday use.)

Since puppies need lots of care, your family has to make a plan to share the work fairly. Who will give it food and water? Who will take it for walks when it's older? Who is going to train it?

Where will your puppy live when it first arrives home? Young puppies can't control when or where they go to the bathroom, so many people keep them in a corner of the kitchen or another room with smooth flooring that's easy to mop up. You could make or buy a fenced-in "playpen" area for the pup. You could also use a kennel cage. These are good because you can move them from room to room. You can keep your puppy close to you at night, and move it to another part of the house during the day.

Here are a few more things you need to have ready for your new dog.

1. **Food and water bowls.** Plastic dishes cost less than other kinds, but once they're scratched they're hard to clean. Also, some puppies have jaws that are strong enough to chew these bowls to pieces and they may even swallow some plastic. Stainless steel bowls cost more, but they don't wear out and they're easier to wash.
2. **Dog food.** Puppies need small meals four or five times a day. (For more on feeding your dog, see p. 75.) It's easier on your puppy's digestive system if you stick to the same food it has been eating, at least for a couple of weeks. Many breeders and animal shelters provide a diet sheet when you pick up your puppy.

3. **A bed.** Young puppies chew on everything, so the first bed can be a simple cardboard box. Cut out one side so that the puppy can get in and out. Make sure the sides are high enough to keep out drafts. Put an old soft blanket or towel in the bottom.

4. **A soft leather or nylon collar.** A dog's collar fits when you can slide two fingers into it while it's on the dog's neck. The collar should have a name tag engraved with your family's name and address. Most communities require you to pay for a licence for your dog. This is usually a metal tag with an identification number that the dog wears on its collar.

5. **Dog toys and grooming supplies.** You'll also need some sturdy dog toys that your puppy can't gnaw to pieces, and some grooming supplies. Different dogs need different kinds of brushes. Ask an expert or read a book about your breed's special needs. Later on, you'll need a leash, although puppies should not go for walks until they've had their *vaccinations* (shots), so they won't pick up diseases from other dogs.

When your puppy first arrives home, everyone will be excited about the new pet. But remember that your puppy is a tired baby. It's bewildered by its new surroundings. Approach it gently and quietly at first. When you pick it up, hold it securely. Put one arm under its forelegs and around its middle, and use your other hand to support its hind legs so that they aren't dangling down.

Your puppy may have a few lonely nights before it gets used to its new home. To make its bed more comforting, you could put a hot-water bottle under its blanket. (But make sure the puppy can't get at it, or you may have a chewed bottle and a wet dog in the morning!) A clock that ticks, also wrapped in a towel, seems to soothe a puppy.

At first, your puppy will learn a few house rules about what it can or can't chew and where it should go to the bathroom. As it grows older, your dog should learn to walk on a leash, sit, stay, and come on command. There are many books to help you train your dog, including some written especially for children. There are a few things they all agree on. When your dog does something right, give it lots of praise. When your dog does something wrong, let it know clearly that its behavior isn't acceptable. Never shout at your dog or hit it or scare it. Above all, you and your family have to be *consistent*. This means using the same command words and sticking to your rules all the time, so that your dog knows what to expect. A dog can only be happy if it knows what to do to please you.

Shake a Paw

You probably already think your pet is the smartest dog in the neighborhood. Teach your dog this trick, and everyone else will think so, too!

Things You'll Need:
kindness and patience

1. Have your dog sit facing you. Now say "Shake" and hold out your hand to take one of the dog's front paws. Maybe your dog will give you its paw right away. (Sometimes dogs naturally raise a paw to show that they think you're the boss.) If your dog does give you a paw, make sure it knows you're *really* thrilled.
2. If you don't get the paw, do this: Push your dog gently on one shoulder, just until the dog begins to lose its balance. The dog will lift its paw to balance itself. Grasp the paw and say "Shake." Then shower praise on your pet. Soon it will realize that shaking paws is a terrific thing to do when it wants some human attention.
3. When your dog does this trick well, show it off to your friends and family. They'll all want to shake a paw!

Training Treats

When you are teaching your dog new skills, it's handy to have some small food treats for rewards. These yummy rice balls won't fill up your pet's stomach with empty calories and they won't rot its teeth.

Things You'll Need:

250 mL (1 cup) uncooked long-grain white rice

water

sesame seeds

saucepan for stove or casserole dish that can be used in a microwave oven

stirring spoon

waxed paper

Important: Get your parents' permission before you use the stove or microwave oven.

Regular Stove Instructions:
1. Put the water and the rice in a saucepan. Put the saucepan on the stove and set the burner to high. When the water starts to boil, change the burner heat to a low setting.
2. Put a lid on the saucepan and cook the rice until it's tender and sticky. (This takes about 20 minutes.) Stir the rice from time to time to keep it from sticking to the bottom of the pot.
3. Remove the cover from the pot and leave the rice until it's cool.

Microwave Oven Instructions:

1. Put 550 mL (2-1/4 cups) of water in a microwave-safe casserole dish. Cook the water on the high setting for about 10 minutes or until it boils.
2. Take the casserole dish out of the oven. Measure 250 mL (1 cup) of rice in a measuring cup and stir it into the water.
3. Put the lid back on the casserole and microwave on the medium setting for about 8 minutes, or until the rice is tender and sticky.
4. Remove the cover from the casserole and leave the rice until it's cool enough to handle.

Rolling the Treats:

1. Wet your hands and roll the rice into bite-size balls.
2. Spread sesame seeds on a piece of waxed paper.
3. Roll the rice balls in the seeds. (You should get about a dozen treats.)

Looking Good, Feeling Fine

Does this sound familiar? Your family is eating dinner and Duchess is begging for her share. She looks so sad, gazing at you with her big brown eyes, putting one paw on your leg, even whimpering. She desperately wants some lasagna or chili or chocolate cake, or whatever else you're eating. Be kind to Duchess and don't feed her from the table. If everyone in the family slips little tidbits to her, she may overeat or upset her stomach with food that is too rich or spicy for her.

Dogs can eat table scraps as *part* of their diet. But veterinarians say that people's leftovers shouldn't make up more than one-quarter of a dog's meal. Put the scraps in Duchess's dish and mix it with her own food.

What should Duchess eat? The easiest way to make sure that your dog is getting all the nutrients she needs is to buy food that is canned or packaged especially for dogs. Look for labels that say the food is a "complete diet" or a "balanced diet." Usually dog food labels will also suggest how much to feed your dog. As you can guess, small or slow-moving dogs need less food than big or active dogs. Young puppies usually need about four small meals a day. A six-month-old needs two or three meals a day. A grownup dog only needs one or two meals. Make sure that Duchess has a big spill-proof water dish and keep it filled with fresh, cool water.

If you can't feel Duchess's ribs with your fingers, and if her flesh shakes when she walks, then she is probably too fat. Overweight dogs get sick more often and have shorter lives than trimmer dogs. Talk to your veterinarian about putting Duchess on a diet.

To keep Duchess fit, give her some outdoor exercise every day. In hot weather, walk her early in the morning or after the sun goes down. Toy dogs may only need a walk of about 1 km (half a mile), but big energetic dogs such as Labrador Retrievers may need up to 8 km (5 miles) a day. That sounds like a long way, but a dog can get a lot of exercise just running back and forth after a ball or Frisbee.

Dogs should be brushed from once a day to once a week, depending on their coats. Pet stores sell special combs and brushes for every kind of dog, from fluffy Bichon Frises to sleek-coated Weimaraners. Start when your dog is a puppy and it will learn to look forward to this special attention from you.

Treat Duchess gently when you are grooming her. Never tug on tangles. Hold the tangle close to the roots with your thumb and first finger, so the dog's skin won't be pulled while you separate the hairs. Ask an adult to help you if the tangle must be cut out with scissors.

Once a week, check Duchess's paws to make sure there is nothing stuck between the pads. (In the winter, rinse her paws with warm water after walks so that iceballs and road salt won't hurt her pads.) Use a clean damp cloth to wipe any eye discharge off her face. Check her mouth from time to time to see whether she has decayed teeth or sore, bleeding gums. Nail clipping and ear cleaning — especially important for the floppy-eared breeds — are tricky. Unless someone has shown you exactly what to do, you probably want to leave these jobs to the adults in your family.

Most dogs don't like baths, so you'll probably need help to do the job. Get all your supplies together before you start. You'll need dog shampoo (human shampoo is too harsh for a dog's coat), towels, and a rinsing scoop or pail. Put a nonskid mat in the bottom of the bathtub or use a plastic wash basin. Fill the tub or basin with warm water (not hot) about halfway up Duchess's legs. Wet her coat and then shampoo her all over, starting from her neck and working back. Do her head last. Rinse her well, making sure to keep suds out of her eyes. Dry Duchess with a towel or use a hairdryer on the low setting. Even after her coat seems dry, though, don't let her go outside for three or four hours. Unless Duchess is really filthy, try to avoid giving her baths in the winter when she might catch a cold. Instead, you can buy dry shampoos at pet stores that will clean her without water.

Your family should make sure Duchess gets her *vaccinations* (shots). Vaccinations protect a dog from diseases that could kill it, such as *distemper* (a disease something like pneumonia) and *parvovirus* (like very bad stomach flu). A veterinarian will usually start to give a puppy its shots when it's about eight weeks old. Once the dog is grown up, it should get annual booster shots. Keep a record of all the shots your dog has had.

A dog should also see a veterinarian if it seems sick. According to the Toronto Humane Society, here are some things to watch for:

1. Your dog won't eat for several days
2. It is coughing a lot
3. It seems very tired and just wants to lie around
4. It is much thirstier than usual
5. Its eyes or nose are runny
6. Its bowel movements are runny or bloody
7. It *vomits* (throws up) more than once, especially on an empty stomach
8. It has a *convulsion* (shakes all over)
9. It has a sore place it doesn't want you to touch
10. It is constantly scratching itself.

When your dog is showing any of these symptoms, take it to a vet right away. Next to you, a veterinarian is your dog's best friend.

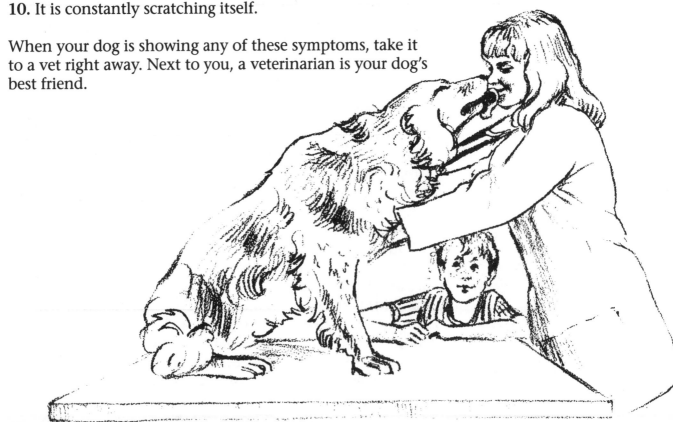

CHOW FOR CHAMPIONS

Many supermarkets have a whole aisle of nothing but pet food. With so much to choose from, how do you buy the right food for your dog? The Canadian Veterinary Medical Assocation has a free booklet to help you decide. It explains why dogs and cats shouldn't eat each other's food, why most dogs don't need vitamin pills, and why you shouldn't feed your pet table scraps.

Write to:
The CVMA Food Certification Program
339 Booth Street
Ottawa, Ontario
K1R 7K1

Ask for: A Commonsense Guide to Feeding Your Dog and Cat

Don't Forget: Print your own address clearly on your letter, so that the CVMA will know where to send your booklet.

SURPRISING FACTS ABOUT DOGS

Deadly Snacks

We've all seen pictures of dogs gnawing happily on bones. Many people think of them as the nicest gifts they can give their pets. But some bones can injure or even kill a dog. Small, sharp chicken or fish bones can pierce a dog's mouth or digestive system. Round bones can get stuck in a dog's throat. Big, thick bones are safer, but dogs with strong jaws may still crush them into dangerous splinters. Fake bones and rawhide chews from pet stores are usually a better choice than real bones. Check with your veterinarian about the right kind of chewy treat for your dog.

The other dangerous treat for dogs is chocolate. People are usually surprised to hear this. After all, many dogs beg for pieces of candy when they see humans enjoying them. But dogs are very sensitive to a chemical in chocolate called *theobromine*. It makes them vomit, gives them diarrhea, and can even kill them. Just 113 g (4 oz.) of chocolate—that's about the amount in a large chocolate bar —can poison a medium-sized dog.

Flee-Away-Flea Biscuits

Some dog experts suggest that you can make your dog less appealing to fleas by adding brewer's yeast and garlic to its diet. See if it works for your pet.

500 mL (2 cups) all-purpose flour

125 mL (1/2 cup) wheat germ

125 mL (1/2 cup) brewer's yeast (you can get this at a health food store)

5 mL (1 tsp.) salt

1 clove garlic, minced

45 mL (3 tbsp.) vegetable oil

250 mL (1 cup) chicken stock (homemade or buy it canned at the grocery store)

medium and large mixing bowls

mixing spoon

measuring spoons

2 large baking sheets

(an electric mixer makes the mixing go faster)

Important: Get your parents' permission before you use the oven.

1. Set the oven to 200° C (400° F) .
2. Lightly oil the baking sheets. Do this by pouring a little vegetable oil on the baking sheets and spreading it around with your fingers.

3. In the medium mixing bowl, mix together the flour, wheat germ, brewer's yeast, and salt.
4. In the large mixing bowl, combine the garlic, chicken broth, and vegetable oil.
5. Add about a third of the flour mixture to the large bowl. Stir it well. Beat it with an electric mixer or stir it with a spoon until it's well mixed.
6. Add another third of the flour. Beat or stir the mixture again. Then add the final third and mix until the batter is smooth.
7. Shape the dough into a ball with your hands.
8. Sprinkle a little flour on a cutting board. With a rolling pin, roll out the dough until it's about 1 cm (1/2 inch) thick. Use a cookie cutter about 5 cm (2 ins.) across to cut out the dog biscuits. (If you don't have a cookie cutter, use a glass or other kitchen container that has a rim about 5 cm (2 ins.) across. Dip the cutter in flour from time to time to keep it from sticking in the biscuit dough.
9. Put the biscuits on the oiled baking sheets.
10. Bake the biscuits in the oven for about 25 minutes, or until they're golden brown. Then *turn off the oven* and leave the biscuits in the oven to dry out for a couple of hours.
11. This recipe makes about 36 biscuits. You can store them in the refrigerator or freezer until they're needed.

You can also try sprinkling a little brewer's yeast on your dog's regular food to help keep the fleas away. Some dogs don't like the taste of brewer's yeast, so sprinkle very lightly.

Dog Gone!

Every few weeks, a new sign goes up in my neighborhood. It usually says something like this: "Lost: Male Golden Retriever. Answers to the name of Lucky. No collar or tags. Please call 555-6666." For every sign, there is an anxious family. For every sign, there is a lost and bewildered pet. How can you keep your dog from getting lost? And, if your dog does wander off, how can you get it back?

Your dog should never be allowed to run around the neighborhood alone. Dogs on their own, even a good dog like yours, can get into mischief. They can scare people who are uneasy around dogs, even when they only want to play. They can leave their droppings on sidewalks and lawns. They can dig up flower beds. Dogs can poison themselves by chewing their way into someone's garbage. They may dart into the path of a car.

In many places it is against the law to let your dog run loose. Someone who sees your dog roaming may call the local animal control department to come and pick it up. Then your dog will find itself in an animal shelter, and your family may have to pay a fine to get it back.

When you take your dog for a walk, it should be on a leash. Is your dog well-trained to come when it's called? Then it might be all right to let your dog run in a field or an uncrowded park where dogs are allowed. Check with your parents before you do this. But what if your dog only comes when there's nothing more interesting to do? Then you're taking a big chance when you unsnap the leash. If your dog sees a cat or a squirrel or even another dog, your pet might be off in a flash. Your dog can romp safely in your backyard, if the yard has a fence strong enough and high enough to keep the dog in.

Even careful pet owners can make a mistake or be unlucky. It's good to be prepared just in case you ever lose

Polished Performance

Shiloh the Collie was missing! Soon after the Brown family moved into their new home in Plantation, Florida, their pet wandered off. They searched for hours, but there was no sign of Shiloh. Then Susan Brown remembered that Shiloh liked to push his head against furniture while she was dusting it with lemon-scented polish. Susan got out the polish and took a walk through her new neighborhood. Every once in a while, she sprayed a little polish on the sidewalk to make a scent trail. Within 15 minutes, Shiloh picked up the lemon scent and found his way home!

your dog. Take a clear photograph of your pet that you could use on a missing poster. Make sure your dog always wears its collar and identification tags. Your family might also want to consider the Infopet system. A veterinarian injects your dog with a tiny microchip, the size of a grain of rice. There's a special 10-digit code on the microchip that identifies the pet and its owners. Veterinarians and animal shelters use a special scanner to read the chip of a lost dog.

If the sad day ever comes when your dog is lost, swing into action right away. Tell all the people you know in your neighborhood that your dog is missing. Call your local animal shelter to find out if your dog has been taken there. Be ready to give the shelter a full description of your dog. They will want to know its breed, sex, age and name. Mention anything else about your dog that makes it easy to spot. Does it have a limp, for instance? If you live in a small community, you could ask the police to keep an eye out for your dog while they're on patrol.

Make a poster like the one on p. 84. Post copies of it in your neighborhood at least five blocks in all directions from where your dog was lost. Put posters up on the bulletin board at your school and at local stores. Check the veterinary clinics in your area. If your dog was injured, someone might have taken it to a veterinarian. If your dog was purebred, and especially if it was tattooed, phone the Canadian Kennel Club. People often call the CKC to let them know they've found a tattooed dog.

Check the Lost and Found column in the newspaper to see if your dog is listed. If a few days go by with no word of your pet, ask your parents to run an ad in that column. In the meantime, keep looking. Lost pets sometimes turn up weeks or months after they disappear.

LOST

Have you seen Gizmo?

Gizmo was last seen July 9 near the
playground in Swift Creek Park.

DESCRIPTION:

1-year-old male German Shepherd-Labrador cross,
wearing red bandanna that says "I brake for cats"
Licence Tag No. 12345-0

If you find Gizmo, please call 333-0000, after 5:00 P.M.

Safety note: If someone calls to say your dog has been
found, *do not* invite this person to come to your home
unless an adult can be there with you. And *never* go to a
stranger's house unless an adult goes with you.

On the Road With Wroofus

Summer vacation is finally here, and you're going on a camping trip! Can your Labrador Retriever (or Cairn Terrier or Dachshund) go with you? Sure, if your dog is fit and healthy, and you follow a few guidelines.

Before you leave, check ahead to make sure that pets are welcome at the campgrounds where you plan to stay. Your family should also make sure that your dog has had all the vaccinations it needs. Take the vaccination and health certificates along with you, especially if you'll be crossing a border into another country. Ask your veterinarian to recommend a flea and tick repellent. Finally, make sure that your dog's collar has an identification tag on it that gives your family name, address, and phone number. If you know where you'll be staying, put your vacation address on the tag, too.

Wroofus will feel more relaxed on the road and at the campground if you bring along his favorite things. This includes his water bowl and food dish, his favorite blanket or cushion, and his toys.

What about feeding him? To keep dogs from getting carsick, many veterinarians suggest that you don't feed them for a few hours before you leave. (You will give Wroofus water to drink, of course.) On the road, dry dog food is handy because it doesn't need a refrigerator. If you use small cans of dog food, you won't have leftovers to worry about. Take along some cool water in a big thermos jug, so that Wroofus can have a drink whenever he's thirsty.

How should a dog travel in the car? It's best for small dogs to travel in a pet carrier. Make sure that fresh air can get into it and that the dog is comfortable inside. Bigger dogs can lie across the back seat if they're well trained and will stay quiet. We've all seen dogs hanging out of car windows as they speed down the highway. They look happy and excited with their ears blown back by the wind, and they probably are. But if an insect or a piece of grit collides with their eyes or ears, it will hurt a lot.

There's an even bigger danger for dogs in cars—summer heat. Often people leave their dog in the car when they stop to eat or shop. "We won't be long," they think. "Anyway, the car's in the shade, and we've left the window open a bit so the dog can get some air." People take longer than they think they will. The patch of shade moves, leaving the car in the sun. And even with the window open, a car can heat up to 50° C (120° F) in just three minutes. This is hot enough to kill your pet.

When you need a food and bathroom stop, Wroofus probably does, too. *Always* put his leash on before you open the car door. Even a well-behaved dog may suddenly bolt away. And give him a chance to exercise before you put him back in the car. Use a short leash for city or gas station stops.

When you finally arrive at the campground, Wroofus will be longing to run and play. Most campgrounds have a rule that dogs have to be on leashes. But even if you're staying somewhere where your dog can run free, it's risky to let him do it. You don't want him to chew on wild plants or mushrooms that could make him sick. And don't let him drink water that has a scum of blue-green algae floating on it. This stuff is very poisonous for your dog.

High-spirited dogs who run off into the woods may meet the local wildlife. A face full of skunk spray or porcupine quills isn't a pleasant start to a holiday! In wilderness areas where there are bears, it's even more important for your family to keep your dog nearby and under control. Put Wroofus on a long leash so that he can romp and explore without getting into any trouble.

The best way to make sure Wroofus enjoys the family vacation is to enjoy it yourself. Sometimes pets are upset by travel and changes in their routine. But when they see their family having a good time, they usually want to join right in. Happy holidays!

How Old Is Your Dog?

How old is your dog in human years? Dogs do most of their growing up in their first year. A one-year-old dog is like a 15-year-old person. At two, a dog is about the same as a 24-year-old person. To find your dog's age after that, add four human years for *each one* of the next four dog years. This means that a dog who is three is like a 28-year-old person; a four-year-old dog is like a 32-year-old, and so on. After the dog reaches six, add five years for each dog year. This means that a 12-year-old dog is roughly as old as a 70-year old person.

Most dogs live about 11 to 15 years. In general, though, big breeds have shorter lifespans than smaller ones. For instance, Irish Wolfhounds are very old at 10, while Fox Terriers may live to be 18 or 20.

Even if you don't know when your dog was born, you can still figure out its age pretty closely by looking at its teeth. At two-and-a-half months, a puppy has only its "*milk teeth*" (a set of 28 baby teeth). By seven months, the dog has a complete set of 32 adult teeth. At one-and-a-half years, the lower middle incisors (the small teeth in the front of the dog's mouth) are a little worn down. By two-and-a-half, all the lower incisors are showing signs of wear. At six years, all the dog's teeth look worn and yellowed, and by ten, the smaller teeth may be worn down to the roots.

There are other signs of old age in dogs. They may move slowly or stiffly. Often, the fur on their faces begins to turn white. Old dogs' eyes may look sunken, as pads of fat build up around them. And finally, they may have *calluses* (patches of thick, rough skin) on their elbows and *hocks* (the jutting ankle bones on their hind legs).

🐾 *Try it Yourself*

Fast Fun With a Frisbee

Does your dog love to race after a ball or stick and bring it back to you? A game with a Frisbee is even more fun.

Before You Start:
Your dog should already be able to play "fetch" with a stick or ball. If it doesn't know how to do this, read some training books to find out how it can learn. There are some dog training books written especially for kids.

Can you make a Frisbee go where you want it to? If not, you need to practice with people before you bring your dog into the act.

Things You'll Need:
a Frisbee that belongs to your dog — pet stores sell tough discs that dogs can't chew to pieces, and they even come in sizes to suit different-sized dogs

a big, open grassy space, away from roads and traffic. (If you go to a park, make sure it's one where dogs and Frisbees are allowed.)

patience — your dog may take a while to learn Frisbee skills

1. Roll the Frisbee on its edge along the ground, toward your dog. Usually the dog will follow its path. At some point, your dog will probably try to grab the Frisbee with its teeth. If your pet stops the Frisbee, give it lots of praise. It the dog actually manages to get the Frisbee in its jaws, praise it even more.
2. Ask your dog to return the Frisbee to you, using whatever command you used when training your dog to fetch.

3. When your dog gets tired of trying to grab the Frisbee, quit for the day.

4. Once your dog is doing a good job of nabbing a rolled Frisbee, it may be time for midair catches. Only healthy dogs with strong hind legs should try this. Crouch down to your dog's level. Throw the Frisbee in a straight line. Urge your dog to fetch it.

5. Get your dog used to jumping for the Frisbee by holding it up in the air while your dog tries to get it. Let your dog "win" often and shower it with praise when it does.

6. If all these stages have gone well, you and your dog are ready for high tosses and flying leaps. You may have seen TV shows about champion Frisbee catchers who make amazing leaps. Remember that those dogs and owners have practiced hard for a long time to get to that stage. If your dog turns out to have a special talent for Frisbee catching, great! If not, remember that the real point is to have a good time with your dog, whether you are Frisbee superstars or not.

Note: Some dogs, like some people, are not great athletes. Some breeds, such as Basset Hounds, aren't built to leap for Frisbees. Pet stores have other good toys for these dogs.

Index